Evolving Through the Way

A Martial Artist's Journey Through Pain, Purpose, and Becoming

Tristan Davis

Davis MAA Publications
Morehead, Kentucky
2025

ISBN: 979-8-9936074-0-5

Disclaimer
The practices and philosophies in this book reflect the author's personal
experience. Martial arts training carries inherent risks. Consult a qualified
instructor or medical professional before attempting any techniques or
beginning any new program. This book is for informational and
inspirational purposes only and is not a substitute for formal instruction
or medical advice. The author and publisher assume no liability for any
injuries or damages resulting from its use.

Scripture quotations are taken from the King James Version of the Bible.
Public domain.

Cover photo by Luka Bowman
Cover design by Rica Graphics

Published by Davis MAA
Printed in the United States of America
First Edition, 2025

Dedication

To my family — the foundation of my strength and the reason I continue this path.

To my parents, for teaching me discipline, respect, and perseverance from day one.

To my brothers, my lifelong training partners — every lesson we learned together became part of who I am today.

And to my students, past, present, and future — you are the reason I keep evolving and your growth continues to inspire mine.

This book is for all who walk the Way with courage, humility, and heart.

Acknowledgments

No journey is ever taken alone, and this one is no exception.

To my father — thank you for introducing me to the Way and showing me that martial arts is more than a skill; it's a way of life.

To my mother — for your patience, your strong support, and your belief in me, whatever the challenge may be. She reminds me that, *"For the LORD is good; his mercy is everlasting; and his truth endureth to all generations"* (*Psalm 100:5, KJV*)

To my brother — for the countless hours of training, challenge, and encouragement. You've been both a rival and a reminder of what it means to grow through discipline.

I also want to thank every student who's ever stepped onto the mat with me. Each of you brought a new lesson, a new perspective, and a new opportunity to learn.

To my instructors and mentors — for your wisdom, your honesty, and your example of leadership through humility.

And finally, to all those who continue to carry the spirit of martial arts into the world: you are proof that the Way is alive, evolving, and endless.

Author's Note

This book isn't about championships, belts or titles. It's about the lessons the dojo — and being a father — continue to teach me every day: patience, discipline, humility, and growth.

Thank you for walking this path with me.
— Tristan Davis

Where the Path Begins

For as long as I can remember, the dojo has been part of my life. I didn't step into martial arts out of curiosity — I was born into it. My earliest memories smell like sweat on the carpet, sound like the sharp snap of a gi, and feel like the quiet focus before bowing in.

Over the years, I've learned that being a martial artist isn't about titles, trophies, or how many belts hang on your wall. It's about what changes inside of you — how you think, how you act, and how you carry yourself when no one's watching.

When I was young, I thought reaching black belt meant I'd made it. Later, I realized it only meant I was ready to start learning the right way. Every experience that followed — victories, failures, teaching, competing, and even the mistakes — taught me that the greatest fight is never against another person. It's the fight to keep growing.

That's what this book is about. It's not about which style is better or who can hit the hardest. It's about evolution — the constant reshaping of body and mind. It's about building confidence that's quiet, not loud. It's about surviving life's hits and coming back smarter, calmer, stronger.

And most of all, it's about giving back — because true martial artists lift others as they climb.

There is no finish line — only the next step. The path deepens, and each time you take that step, you rise.

CHAPTER I

Born Into the Way

✦

Some people choose martial arts.

I didn't. It chose me.

I don't remember the first time I walked into a dojo. Not because it wasn't important, but because it was never a moment—I was simply born into it. Long before I threw a punch or tied my first belt, the sound of snapping gis, Japanese counting, the sharp kiais echoing through the building in unison, and the slap of feet against carpet were just part of the background noise of my childhood.

For most kids, a playground was where they tested their limits. For me, it was the training floor. I learned early that martial arts wasn't a hobby—it was a way of life, a language that taught discipline before I even understood the word.

One of my earliest clear memories wasn't of me training—it was of my father moving like liquid electricity on an old, grainy VHS tape. The picture quality wasn't great, the date in the corner blurry; however, I could see everything that mattered. The way the crowd leaned forward when he bowed in. The precision in his stance. The intensity in his eyes before the first strike. I didn't fully understand what I was looking at, but I understood that this man wasn't just my father in that moment. He was someone people watched. Someone they respected. Someone they believed in.

There were whispered names I would hear as a kid—Chuck Norris, Bill "Superfoot" Wallace, Bruce Lee—names that seemed surreal. Legends. Men whose names were spoken with a certain weight in martial arts. I didn't realize until later that my father had trained alongside some of them. At the time, all I knew was that grown men with black belts in other styles bowed deeper when they greeted him. When he entered a tournament ring, even as a judge or coach, people noticed.

Tournaments took place occasionally on Saturdays. I remember sitting near the judge's table while my father organized divisions, bowing competitors in with calm authority. The room would be filled with anxious energy from fighters warming up, spectators yelling, but he walked through it like someone who already understood the outcome of every match. I didn't know what it meant to be a champion yet, but I knew what it meant to be respected before a match even started. I learned early that respect wasn't given during the fight—it was carried into it.

Growing up in that atmosphere meant I didn't see martial arts as just an extracurricular activity. Some kids went to practice after school; I grew up inside a living, breathing dojo culture. I didn't feel pressured by words—nobody ever sat me down and said I had to be great—but expectations could be felt in the silence created. I wasn't told to carry the family name with pride. I simply saw what it meant early on.

I started training with adults before I was a teenager. It wasn't a ceremony or a test—I had simply reached a point where there were no more kids' classes that challenged me. I remember the first time I heard "fall in" where every student besides me had facial hair. When I bowed in, I could feel their eyes drifting toward me—not cruel, just curious. I was the kid who was born into this. That meant something, even if I didn't know it yet.

I got hit harder in those classes. Not negatively, but because in that room, being young didn't mean being weak. Even though I tried to stand tall and breathe steady, there were moments when my chest tightened with doubt—not fear of getting hurt, but fear of disappointing a standard I didn't fully understand but always felt.

That was my introduction to the martial arts—not as something I chose, but something I stepped into as naturally as breathing. I didn't yet know what "The Way" truly meant. I only knew I was expected to walk it.

FORGED BY THE FLOOR

Training in the early days wasn't diluted for the youth. Students ran laps around the building barefoot for warmup. The dojo floor wasn't covered in thick mats you see these days. It was carpet laid directly over concrete—just enough to hide the hardness underneath, never enough to soften it. When you were swept or dropped during drills, the burn of the carpet hit first, a quick scrape across your skin, followed immediately by the sound that echoed through bone. No one rushed over to ask if you were okay. The expectation wasn't spoken—it was simple: get up and continue.

I didn't resent it. At that age, I didn't even think to question whether it was hard or unfair. It was just *the way things were*. Pain wasn't something to fear; nevertheless, it was something you learned to move through quietly. Looking back, I think the floor taught me before the instructors did. It taught me that this path wasn't cushioned, and neither was life.

There was no ceremony that marked the shift from being a child in the dojo to being treated like someone expected to hold their own. One day, I was lined up in front with the younger students, and the next, I found myself in the adult line. I remember being shorter than everyone around me, my belt barely brushing against the hips of people who had facial hair or long work shifts. I stood among them not because I had earned their level of strength yet, but because I had been born into this environment—and that meant growing into it faster than others.

Nobody told me to be tough. They just trained me the same way they trained everyone else. When I struggled to keep up, no one announced that I was too young. They expected me to adapt. I think that's when I first recognized that I wasn't just being raised in a family—I was being raised in a standard.

I can still remember the sound of adults breathing heavily beside me during drills, their footsteps pounding on the floor, hearing "osu" in the background. My own breath came out shorter and faster, not because I was unwilling, but because my body hadn't yet caught up to the intensity of the room I had been placed in. Still, I pushed. Partly because I wanted to prove I belonged there, and partly because I didn't know another way to exist.

In a strange way, nobody ever told me to "be strong," but everyone around me lived as though there wasn't another option. That kind of environment shapes you in silence. And even though I hadn't chosen this path yet, I was already walking it.

MEASURED AGAINST A SHADOW

As I got older, I started to notice something that I hadn't been aware of before. When I stepped onto the floor, eyes would shift—not aggressively, not with judgment, but with an almost quiet curiosity. It wasn't because of anything I had done. It was because of who my father was.

I didn't fully understand it at the time, but I could feel it. When a drill started, people watched to see *how I would perform it.* When sparring rotations began, my partners gave a split-second pause, as if unsure how hard they were supposed to go. When I struggled, it wasn't just my struggle—it felt like I was being measured against a standard I didn't set.

Nobody said it out loud, but I could sense the unspoken question in the room: *"Is he going to be like his father?"*

At first, I didn't know what to do with that feeling. I wasn't trying to prove anything. I was just trying to learn. But over time, that quiet tension became part of the atmosphere around me. I wasn't just another student—I was *Shihan's son*. Whether or not anyone intended it, that title carried a weight of its own.

I didn't think of it as pressure then. It felt more like a question that followed me onto the floor every day. Was I learning because I loved it—or because I was expected to? Was I pushing to get better—or because I didn't want to fall short of a reputation that didn't belong to me yet?

There were times when I performed well and heard quiet nods of approval or saw small smiles from black belts standing at the edge of the room. Those moments felt good, but they didn't feel like achievements. They felt like confirmation that I hadn't disappointed anyone *that day*.

But when I made mistakes or fell behind in a drill, even if nobody said anything, I could feel my chest tighten—not because I feared failing, but because I feared confirming the thought that maybe I didn't deserve the place I stood in.

That's when I first started to understand that martial arts wasn't just training—it was identity. And identity wasn't something you were given. It was something you either stepped into or walked away from. There was no middle ground. I didn't yet know what my own name meant out on the floor. I only knew that it had already been spoken there long before I was ready to speak for myself. And with that realization, I started to care—not just about doing the techniques right, but about becoming someone worthy of the path I had inherited.

I wasn't just learning martial arts anymore.

I was becoming shaped by them.

WHEN DEFEAT SPOKE LOUDER THAN LEGACY

Tournaments always carried a different kind of energy than the dojo. In class, even the hardest training had a rhythm I recognized—familiar voices, familiar footwork, familiar expectations. But at tournaments, everything felt sharper, louder, more exposed. The gym floors weren't home. The air was full of tension that didn't belong to me alone.

By then, I had already been training with adults, already used to being watched. But stepping into a ring felt different. You weren't just performing a drill—you were being tested. Not for a rank. Not for a promotion. For something you couldn't see but could absolutely feel.

I remember standing in my ring that day, adjusting my gloves, trying to find calm in the sound of my own breathing. My opponent was older, bigger, more experienced. I knew that. Everyone did. I told myself that I wasn't there because I was guaranteed to win—I was there because I was expected to compete. Still, a part of me wondered if people assumed I would somehow rise to my father's name.

The referee called us to bow in. I did it automatically—bowing had become muscle memory by then—but my mind was running faster than my stance. I could hear scattered voices in the crowd, but not clearly enough to make out words. It was just noise, a constant reminder that this moment wasn't private.

When the match started, I tried to stay composed, to find my rhythm. But I was tense. Hesitant. My strikes were measured, maybe too careful, thrown with more thought than instinct. He moved faster than I expected. Harder than I was ready for. I blocked one combination, slipped another, but I was reacting instead of leading, and in sparring, reacting often meant falling behind.

Then it happened—not in slow motion, but in brutal clarity.

He caught me clean. A strike I didn't fully see coming.

My mouthpiece flew out before I even felt the pain. For a moment, everything flashed white. My vision blurred at the edges, and I tasted the metallic edge of adrenaline before blood was even a question. My legs held out of instinct more than strength, but my balance was gone—not just physically, but mentally.

The match ended there for me, even before my opponent officially won. I had been hit before. I had been winded, swept, bruised. But this was different. This wasn't just a strike. This was defeat—public, undeniable, unmissable.

And that's when I heard it.

Not silence.

Cheering.

Not for me.

The cheering hit harder than the strike.

It wasn't a roar meant to celebrate a champion rising—it was a release, like people had been waiting for something, and now they finally got it. Maybe they were cheering for the opponent. Maybe they were just caught in the moment of impact. But standing there, dazed and exposed, it didn't sound like they were celebrating skill. It sounded like they were relieved that I had lost.

My mouthpiece lay on the floor a few feet away, a small reminder that the hit had taken more than just a point. For a moment, the world felt too big and too loud. The edges of the room were blurred shapes. My head was ringing. I couldn't tell if anyone said anything about me, but I felt like every eye in the room had just witnessed me fail to be someone they expected me to be.

I bowed out the same way I always did. I walked back the way I was supposed to. I gave no outward sign that the moment was anything more than a match I didn't win. But inside, something had shifted.

Up until then, even when training was hard, I believed that if I pushed hard enough, if I carried myself right, maybe I really was destined to live up to my father's name—or at least never fall embarrassingly short of it. That hit changed that.

Not because I lost, but because losing didn't feel like something that happened in a moment—it felt like something that echoed. I didn't cry. I didn't break down. I didn't even talk about it later. I just carried it home with me quietly, like a stone in my chest.

In the days after, I kept replaying it—not the match, but the sound of the crowd afterward. It wasn't cruelty that bothered me. It was the realization that I had believed, even a little, that I was unshakeable just because of where I came from.

I wasn't invincible.

I wasn't guaranteed respect just by stepping onto the floor.

And I had no right to think I was beyond being brought down.

In that loss, humility didn't arrive as a lesson someone spoke over me—it entered like a cold breath I couldn't ignore, reminding me that the path I was walking wasn't something I inherited.

It was something I still had to earn.

FROM INHERITANCE TO INTENTION

That loss stayed with me, not as a moment of defeat, but as a quiet shift in awareness. Before that day, I walked onto the floor carrying a name that already meant something to other people. After that day, I understood that a name alone didn't make you anything. If anything, it made you a target.

Humility didn't come to me as a philosophy or a lesson someone explained after class. It came in the form of a strike I didn't block, a mouthpiece I couldn't hold onto, and a crowd that reminded me I wasn't untouchable. But it wasn't humiliation that shaped me—it was the understanding that I still had a long way to go, and that the journey couldn't be walked with ego.

I trained harder after that, not out of fear of losing again, but because I began to see that skill wasn't something anyone inherited. It had to be earned day by day, choice by choice, strike by strike. Being born into martial arts didn't make me a martial artist. It only meant I was placed at the starting line earlier than some. Where I went from there would depend on how I responded to moments like that loss.

There's a difference between being placed on a path and choosing to walk it. From that point on, I started training with a different question in mind—not "Am I as good as people think I should be?" but "Am I growing into someone worthy of this journey?" I didn't gain confidence from that loss. I gained perspective. And perspective, I would later learn, is what separates someone who practices martial arts from someone who lives by them.

At that age, I didn't know the full meaning of humility, discipline, or perseverance. I didn't understand the depth of what I was being taught. But I did know this: the way forward would not be about proving that I belonged because of where I came from—it would be about proving to myself that I was willing to evolve, no matter how many times I was tested.

And that led to my next realization.

The first belt you earn doesn't define you.

Not any more than your name does.

"You are not shaped by the belt you wear,
but by the discipline you carry."

CHAPTER II

The First Belt Doesn't Define You

◆

When you grow up in martial arts from an early age, belt promotions can feel like they're built into your life. I don't remember the day I earned my first belt as a kid with the kind of clarity I later remembered my first true tests. Back then, earning a belt felt less like a breakthrough and more like the expected next step. You participated, you tried your best, you lined up, your name was called, you received a diploma, and someone tied a new color around your waist. Adults clapped, judges nodded with approval, and you bowed with the rest of the class. It was a system, a cycle, a pattern—earn, advance, repeat.

I understood that belts represented progress, but I didn't yet understand growth. I wore them with pride, but not with depth. When I received my black belt as a kid, it carried more weight, but even then, the weight came more from the reactions of others than from my own internal understanding. To many people, a black belt symbolized mastery. To a child raised in the system, it felt like reaching a milestone that had always been waiting for me, almost like graduating from something I hadn't fully realized I was still learning.

People looked at me differently once I earned it—but I wasn't different yet. I still made mistakes. I still had fears. I still had days where my "Mawashi Geri" felt heavy, my spirit tired, and my discipline wavered. The belt didn't erase any of that. It didn't make me sharper, calmer, or wiser overnight. It only made me more noticeable.

What I didn't realize then was that a belt doesn't transform you—it calls you to transformation. It doesn't define you—you have to grow into it. At that age, though, I didn't know that yet. I still thought achievement spoke louder than humility. I still thought reaching a rank meant I had already arrived somewhere.

Later, I would learn that no belt, not even black, is the end of anything. It only confirms that you're ready to begin the real work.

PROMOTION BEFORE TRANSFORMATION

At that age, I thought progression was proof. Proof that I was doing something right. Proof that I belonged. Proof that each step forward meant I was becoming someone stronger, more skilled, maybe even closer to being "complete." Looking back, I realize I treated each new belt like a finish line, even if I didn't say it out loud. There was a silent belief that once you earned the next color, you had reached some new version of yourself—automatically, instantly, by virtue of the rank alone.

The truth was that my kicks didn't magically sharpen the moment the belt changed. My endurance didn't suddenly increase just because the belt on my waist said I should be better now. I still struggled with fatigue. I still hesitated at times when I should've moved with confidence. I still got frustrated when my body wasn't yet capable of executing what I pictured in my mind.

There's a quiet kind of confusion that comes when your outward progress doesn't immediately match your inward growth. As a child, I couldn't explain it, but I felt it. Why didn't I feel as advanced as the color I wore suggested I should be? Why did the belt feel heavier some days, not in weight, but in expectation?

I began to notice something: the higher the rank, the less praise I received for simply showing up. Lower belts were encouraged just for trying. Higher belts were expected to have been there. Somewhere along the line, recognition shifted into responsibility.

Even then, I didn't fully grasp what that responsibility meant. A rank could change how people looked at me, but it couldn't change how prepared I actually was—or wasn't. That tension between appearance and reality would follow me for years before I understood how to close the gap.

Only later would I learn that earning a belt is not the moment you become someone new. It's the moment you're asked to develop into someone new.

SEEN AS COMPLETE, STILL BECOMING

As I moved into higher ranks, something shifted—not in my technique at first, but in what others seemed to expect from me. The praise that came easily when I was younger began to fade, replaced by a quieter observation. Mistakes weren't corrected with the same gentle encouragement they once were. Corrections carried a different tone now—more direct, less forgiving. It wasn't harsh, just... expected.

Once I reached black belt as a kid, the room no longer treated me like someone who was still learning, even though I was. Students with lower ranks assumed I had answers. Some watched me during kata or sparring rounds, studying me not as a peer but as a reference point. Whether I understood it or not, I had crossed into a different category. I was no longer just a student on the path—I was someone others believed had already found his footing on it.

But the truth was, I didn't fully understand what it meant to wear a black belt yet. There's a strange kind of pressure that comes when you are seen as advanced before you feel that way inside. I knew techniques, I knew routines, I knew how to perform. But understanding why certain movements demanded discipline beyond mechanics—that would take years, experience, and struggle. At that time, I was still learning that discipline isn't about what you do when others are watching, but how you carry yourself when no one is praising or pushing you.

The higher I climbed, the more it felt like belts weren't just markers of what I had done, but expectations of who I was supposed to be. I wasn't simply wearing rank anymore—I was wearing perception.

In time, I began to realize there were two versions of myself: the one people believed a black belt should be, and the one still figuring out how to grow into that identity. That gap between how I was seen and who I truly was became a quiet source of internal pressure. I didn't speak about it then, but I felt it every time I tied that belt around my waist.

At a certain point, I understood that a belt could elevate you in the eyes of others long before it elevated your understanding of yourself. And if you weren't careful, it could become a place to settle rather than a place to grow from.

BLACK BELT IN ONE ROOM, WHITE BELT IN ANOTHER

With time and continued dedication, I advanced further, eventually earning higher Dan rankings in my main style. On paper, I had become someone others would now call "sensei." I could teach advanced students, guide classes, and carry conversations about philosophy and application. People outside the dojo respected the rank. Inside the dojo, newer students bowed more deeply. Parents referred to me with a certain tone of pride when they told others where their children trained.

Externally, everything suggested I had become what a martial artist was supposed to be at that level. Internally, though, something quiet had settled in—a kind of familiarity that bordered on comfort. I knew the movements. I knew the expectations. I knew the rhythm of the style I had lived in for so long. And comfort, when mixed with recognition, can start to feel like mastery if it goes untested for too long.

I didn't realize it then, but I was reaching a plateau—not because I lacked motivation, but because I was surrounded by a world that already knew who I was. It's easy to feel complete when no one is asking you to start over. It's easy to believe your belt still defines you when no one is challenging what still lies beneath it.

That began to change when I stepped into Brazilian Jiu-Jitsu (BJJ) training for the first time—not as a black belt, not as a teacher, not as someone expected to know, but as a white belt in a room where nobody cared what rank I held elsewhere.

It was a strange feeling to walk onto a mat after so many years of being looked at as someone who had already "arrived," only to realize I was entering a space where none of that mattered. No one was impressed by the color of my belt from another style. No one assumed I knew anything. And more importantly, I quickly understood that in this room, I *didn't* know anything yet—not in the way that counted here.

I didn't lose respect by stepping in as a beginner again—but I did shed a layer of identity I had gotten used to. And in doing so, I rediscovered what it felt like to truly earn progress rather than inherit expectation.

WHERE REPUTATION ENDED AND EFFORT BEGAN

Starting BJJ as a white belt after earning high Dan rankings elsewhere wasn't humiliating—it was disorienting in a quieter, more personal way. I was used to stepping out on the floor with a level of certainty. My body knew how to respond in familiar patterns. My instincts were trained around timing and movement I had lived in for years. But in Jiu-Jitsu, that instinct meant almost nothing.

Suddenly, the ground was an unfamiliar conversation. My balance didn't translate the same way. Movements I had mastered standing up didn't work once tangled on the mat. I wasn't just a beginner—I was a beginner with habits from another art that didn't always help me here. And the odd thing was, no one cared who I had been in another room. There was no pressure to impress—but there was nowhere to hide either.

There's a different kind of honesty that lives at the bottom of a new system. When you can't rely on reputation, you only have effort. When you can't lean on memory, you must lean on humility. Struggling as a white belt in BJJ didn't make me question whether I was a black belt in my original art—but it did make me realize how long it had been since I had truly felt like a beginner in the purest sense.

Being submitted by someone lower-ranked in my first art would have shaken my pride. Being submitted by someone more skilled in BJJ didn't hurt my pride—it reminded me that the journey was bigger than one style or one rank. It reminded me that even black belts still bleed, breathe, and break.

And somewhere in that initial discomfort, I started to feel something I hadn't felt in a while—a hunger to grow that wasn't tied to expectation or legacy. I didn't want to succeed because people were watching. I wanted to succeed because I had stepped into a place where knowledge wasn't assumed—it had to be earned again from the ground up.

That's when I truly understood:

A belt shows where you've been.
A struggle shows where you're going.

I didn't realize it then, but the discomfort of starting over wasn't meant to weaken me—it was preparing me for something far more defining than a test or a rank.

THE SPACE BETWEEN RANKS

When I think back to earning belts as a kid, they felt like markers of completion. They were milestones that said, *"You've reached this level."* What I understand now is that belts don't declare mastery—they challenge you to begin living up to the expectations tied to them.

My childhood belts represented progress without full understanding. My black belt as a youth gave me confidence, but it didn't yet give me perspective. The higher ranks that followed gave me authority, but they also built a quiet comfort that could have trapped me if I never sought discomfort again.

A belt doesn't change who you are—it tests who you are willing to become. It doesn't make you stronger—it exposes whether you can stay disciplined long enough to embody the strength it represents.

In the end, my first belt didn't define me. Neither did my black belt. Neither did my blue belt in BJJ. What defined me were the moments between those belts—the quiet decisions to stay in the fight, to show up again after losing, to start over without ego, and to push through pain not to earn rank, but to honor the journey.

Belts fade. Colors change. But the mindset you build... that stays with you. Because mastery isn't found in reaching a belt. It's found in learning what it takes to become worthy of wearing it.

"The first time you are asked to lead is rarely the moment you feel ready. But readiness comes from stepping forward, not waiting."

CHAPTER III

Teaching Before Knowing

I didn't fully understand what responsibility felt like until the day I was asked to teach someone who was older than me. I had been promoted to black belt at a young age, and while that rank gave me confidence, it also placed me in situations I wasn't emotionally prepared for. One of those moments came when an instructor looked at me during class and said, "Take them to the side and go over the basics."

Them—in this case—wasn't a group of younger kids or nervous white belts close to my own age. It was a pair of adult students. Grown men. New to the art, unsure in their footing, but older, stronger, and heavier than I was. When I motioned for them to follow me, they did, but not without hesitation in their eyes. They respected the belt I wore, but they clearly questioned the body wearing it.

There's a certain silence that hangs in the air when you're expected to lead before you're sure why you should be leading. I wasn't afraid of teaching the material—I knew the basics inside and out. What unsettled me was the realization that I needed to not only perform them well, but *explain* them in a way that made sense to people who did not yet trust my authority.

They stood in front of me, arms loosely folded, waiting to be taught. I could feel their guarded curiosity—not hostile, but cautious, like they were still deciding whether they should take instruction from someone young enough to be their student in any other context. And for a moment, I felt like I was tied between two identities: a black belt who was expected to know, and a kid who still wasn't fully sure what it meant to teach.

I took a breath and started with the basics—stances, foot positioning, balance. Basics are supposed to be universal, easy to explain. But when you're teaching someone older than you, every word feels like it needs to be more precise, every explanation more justified. I demonstrated the stance slowly, then broke it down in phases—where the weight should sit, why proper rotation in the hips mattered, how tension in the wrong place could throw everything off.

At first, they followed out of courtesy. Their movements were hesitant and their attention slightly distant, as if they were still waiting to see whether what I said had real value. But as I corrected a foot angle here, shifted a knee there, and explained how a good base led to stability, something subtle started to change. They adjusted with more focus. Their posture sharpened. Questions that began as cautious became curious. They weren't just following along with movements anymore—they were trying to understand them.

There's a moment when students stop performing and start learning. I saw it happen in their eyes—the slight shift from skepticism to interest. They weren't looking at me as a kid anymore. They were looking at someone who could help them improve.

That realization didn't instantly make me feel like a teacher. It made me aware of how fragile respect is when you're leading. You don't demand it—you earn it, one clear explanation or insightful correction at a time.

The first real breakthrough came when one of the adults paused during a drill, adjusted his footing, and asked, "Why does the back knee stay slightly bent instead of locking out?" It wasn't a challenge—it was a real question. Not "prove me wrong," but "help me understand." That one question told me something had changed. I wasn't being sized up anymore. I was being listened to. Complete focus was on me.

I explained how keeping the knee slightly bent preserved balance, allowed faster movement, improved flexibility, and prevented stiffness from becoming a weakness during transitions. He nodded, tried it again, and immediately felt the difference. The other student noticed and adjusted as well. From there, more questions came—about hip alignment, weight distribution, reaction timing. They weren't just following—they were trusting the direction.

By the time we moved through the last set of basics, the skepticism in their expressions had faded. When we bowed to end the lesson, they didn't walk away like they had just completed a random drill—they walked away like they had learned something, and they chose to learn it from me.

That experience didn't make me feel accomplished. It made me feel accountable. Knowing the material had been enough to earn a belt—but explaining it well enough to earn respect was something else entirely. I didn't leave that moment thinking, *I am a good teacher now.* I left thinking, *I need to understand even more, because someone might ask again—and next time, I want to be ready.*

In that moment, I realized that teaching isn't about being above someone else—it's about being responsible for what you pass on.

After that class ended, I didn't walk away feeling like I had arrived as an instructor. Instead, I walked away more aware of how much responsibility came with being seen as one. It was the first time I felt a quiet sense of pressure—not from my instructors, not from the other students, but from myself. I didn't just want to show the right techniques anymore. I wanted to *deserve* the trust that someone placed in me when they asked a question expecting clarity. I wanted to give that clarity with confidence.

That day revealed something I hadn't yet considered: when you teach, your understanding is exposed. It's easy to perform a technique by habit, but explaining *the application* forces you to face the gaps in your own knowledge. And in that moment, I realized how much I had been relying on repetition rather than comprehension.

Teaching had turned into a mirror—one that reflected both what I knew and what I didn't. That mirror didn't judge me, but it challenged me. If students were going to look to me for direction, then I needed to keep sharpening not just my physical technique, but my ability to translate understanding into guidance.

I was just a kid with a black belt, but now I understood something I hadn't before. A belt might give you permission to instruct—but it doesn't give you the depth to guide others unless you continue earning that role every time you teach.

From that experience forward, I began to train differently. I was no longer practicing purely for execution—I was practicing for explanation. It wasn't enough to be able to *do* the movement; therefore, I needed to know how to break it down step by step, why it mattered, and how to adjust it for someone who didn't move like me. I started paying closer attention to details I may have let slip before—hand placement, timing of breath, how pressure and relaxation alternated through each technique.

I found myself asking questions during my own training, not because I doubted the technique, but because I wanted to understand it deeply enough to teach it with confidence. Teaching had forced me to confront a truth I hadn't yet realized:

You can't lead someone deeper than you are willing to go yourself.

In the past, earning a belt felt like a personal achievement. After that moment with the adults, each belt I wore—even the one I had already earned—felt like a commitment. Not a symbol of what I had done, but a reminder of what I still needed to live up to.

I didn't suddenly feel prepared to be a teacher. If anything, teaching made me more aware of how much I still had to learn. But it also awakened something within me—a sense of purpose that extended beyond my own performance. I was no longer just trying to be better for myself. I was trying to be better so I wouldn't fail the people who might one day look to me for guidance.

Teaching wasn't making me feel stronger—it was making me feel responsible. And in that responsibility, I began to understand a new kind of growth: one that didn't come from ego or achievement, but from service and accountability.

The more I was asked to help others, the more I started questioning myself—not out of uncertainty, but out of a growing awareness that someone else's progress might now depend on how clearly I could communicate what I knew. There's a different kind of pressure that comes with knowing that someone may repeat a technique incorrectly not because they failed, but because I failed to explain it well.

I didn't express these thoughts to anyone. On the outside, I did what was expected of me—demonstrated, explained, corrected. But internally, I carried a silent question:

Am I good enough to guide someone without leading them in the wrong direction?

That question followed me, not in fear, but in responsibility. It was the beginning of understanding that teaching isn't just about passing knowledge forward—it's about protecting the integrity of the path you're guiding someone down.

Over time, teaching small portions of class trained me in ways I didn't expect. It sharpened my attention. It made me disciplined even when I didn't feel like it. It forced me to stay consistent, because I couldn't tell someone else to be disciplined if I allowed myself to drift. I realized that when people watch you for guidance, they aren't always listening to what you say—they're observing who you are.

And that changed how I approached training, not because I wanted to look good in front of others, but because I understood that my example might become someone else's standard. Teaching before I fully understood my own journey didn't make me feel like a master—it made me feel accountable to becoming a better student.

Looking back, that day didn't turn me into a teacher—but it made me realize that teaching is not a role you step into once you know enough. It's a process that reveals how much more you still must learn. I didn't leave the floor feeling powerful. I left feeling responsible.

Something changed in me quietly after that. I began to see every technique not just as a tool to execute, but as a lesson I might one day have to explain. I started training not only to refine my own ability, but to prepare for the possibility that someone else might need me to help them understand theirs.

Teaching didn't make me feel like I had reached the top of the mountain—it made me understand there's always a higher mountain to climb. And even though I had worn the black belt for some time already, this was one of the first moments I realized that rank does not bring mastery. It invites you to live up to it.

I didn't understand everything yet. I didn't know how much deeper martial arts would push me. But that day shaped a part of my path. It taught me that being seen as a leader before you feel ready doesn't mean you're supposed to have all the answers—it means you're being called to grow into someone who is willing to seek them.

From that point on, I no longer trained just to improve. I trained to understand—and to one day be worthy of passing that understanding on.

BECOMING A LEADER BEFORE KNOWING I WAS ONE

As time went on, being asked to help others didn't feel like a one-time responsibility anymore. It became something I was regularly trusted to do. I found myself stepping to the front of smaller groups or being pulled aside with new students when instructors knew they needed more individualized guidance. At first, I still carried a quiet sense of awareness that I was younger than many of the people I was leading. But the more I explained techniques, the less I thought about my age, and the more I focused on whether my explanations made sense.

Teaching didn't make me question whether I understood what I was doing—it made me realize just how much I actually did understand. The

24

moment someone asked *why* a certain movement needed to be timed a specific way, or what would happen if the stance shifted even slightly, I had to break the technique apart step by step. And the more I broke it down for them, the more clearly I understood it myself.

It became clear that knowing how to execute a technique was one thing—but being able to explain its purpose and application added a level of certainty I hadn't experienced when I was only performing it from memory or habit. I didn't feel like I was losing footing by teaching—I felt like I was solidifying it.

As questions grew deeper, my answers became sharper, and with that came a new kind of confidence. Not an arrogant belief that I had mastered everything, but a grounded assurance that I truly understood the fundamentals I was passing on. I was still very much a student, but teaching made me a more intentional one—someone who trained with purpose, knowing that I might one day be responsible for helping someone else make sense of the same movements.

Over time, I started to realize that people weren't just listening to what I said when I taught—they were watching how I trained when I wasn't teaching. That awareness had a quiet impact on me. I could no longer move through drills on autopilot or let my focus drift just because no one was actively evaluating me. If I was going to correct someone else's form or remind them to tighten their stance, I felt a responsibility to ensure there was never a moment someone could look at mine and quietly think, *"But he doesn't do it himself."*

That wasn't something anyone said out loud. No instructor pulled me aside and told me to live up to the role I was starting to step into. It was something I felt on my own simply by being in front of others. The more I taught, the more aware I became that people learned just as much from what I demonstrated as from what I explained. I began training with sharper focus—not because I wanted to look impressive, but because I didn't want to be careless with the trust others had put in my guidance.

Teaching forced consistency. I couldn't just perform well on the days I felt strong or motivated. I had to be steady—mentally, physically, and even emotionally. If I expected others to stay composed when frustrated, I had to show calm under pressure. If I told someone to keep their hands up when tired, I couldn't drop mine when fatigue set in.

Even though I was still learning the deeper philosophies of martial arts, I was already beginning to understand something important: long before you are formally recognized as a leader, people start learning from you. Sometimes you are teaching even when you don't mean to be—simply by the way you move, focus, breathe, or recover from mistakes.

In those moments, I realized that being seen as an instructor wasn't about being perfect—it was about being consistent in how I approached the journey.

As I continued working with students, I started noticing small things I hadn't paid much attention to before. When I corrected someone's stance, they didn't just adjust—they mimicked the exact way I positioned my feet. When I repeated a technique more slowly, they didn't only follow the motion; they matched my rhythm, my breathing, even the way I reset my posture afterward. Without fully meaning to, I had become a reference point.

At first, that realization was surprising. I thought people were just learning the movement, but I began to see that they were learning my version of it. Everything I did was being absorbed—my pace, my focus, even the way I recovered from mistakes. If I brushed off an error too casually, they did the same. If I worked through it with attention and correction, they mirrored that as well.

There was a moment when a younger student, after making a mistake during a drill, took a breath, reset calmly, and tried again with quiet determination. I recognized the sequence immediately—it looked exactly like how I handled my own missteps in training. And it made me pause, not in pride, but in awareness. I hadn't told him to respond that way—he saw me do it and adopted it himself.

That moment changed something in me. It made me realize that teaching wasn't just about explaining techniques; furthermore, it was about embodying what they meant. Students didn't just listen to instruction—they absorbed attitude. They learned how to stand, but also how to respond after being knocked off balance.

That kind of influence came with a weight of responsibility that felt different than any belt I had ever worn. A belt could identify my rank—but the way I carried myself could shape someone else's journey. I couldn't force them to grow, but I could affect whether they believed growth was worth pursuing.

And that made me take the role more seriously, not because I was certain I was ready to lead—but because I never wanted to be the reason someone settled for anything less than the maximum of their potential.

Realizing that students mirrored not just my movement but my mindset brought a different kind of pressure—one I didn't talk about, but felt every time I stepped onto the floor. It made me more intentional, not just in what I demonstrated, but in how I carried myself when things didn't go smoothly.

There were days when I felt off—when my timing wasn't sharp or fatigue set in early. Before, I might have pushed through quietly or let the feeling pass without much thought. But once I understood others were learning from more than just my victories, I became conscious of how I responded to struggle. If I let frustration show in my posture, someone else might think frustration was how they were supposed to respond too. If I gave less effort on a tough day, it could give someone permission to do the same.

I didn't feel like a master. I didn't even feel like a true instructor yet. But I did start to recognize something important: being watched meant being responsible—not for being perfect, but for being consistent enough that others could trust the way I approached growth.

There's an unspoken stage in every martial artist's journey when they begin leading without ever being told they are a leader. No ceremony marks the moment. No belt is awarded for it. It begins the first time someone adjusts their effort because of you, or holds their head higher because you showed them how to recover with dignity after failing.

That kind of influence doesn't wait for you to declare yourself ready. It appears quietly, and when it does, you either grow into it—or risk being careless with the impact you leave on others. I wasn't fully confident yet, but I was becoming aware. And awareness was the beginning of responsibility. Teaching before truly knowing didn't expose weakness in me—it revealed a call to maturity I hadn't expected yet.

The more I helped others, the more my training shifted from routine to responsibility-driven refinement. I didn't just practice to improve anymore—I practiced to ensure my understanding was strong enough to support those who might rely on it later. Teaching didn't make me feel like I was above others; it made me feel like I had to go deeper than I ever had before, even into familiar techniques.

There's a difference between training to perform and training to guide. When you train to perform, you focus on what your body can do. When you train to guide, you focus on why it works, when it fails, and how to adjust it for someone who moves differently than you. That shift added depth to my approach. I became more attentive to timing, leverage, and intent—not because I was trying to prove I knew everything, but because I didn't want to pass on shallow understanding.

This didn't make me feel like an expert. In fact, it made me increasingly aware of how much I still had to learn. But instead of that awareness being discouraging, it grounded me. I wasn't chasing progress for recognition anymore. I was chasing clarity—for myself and for those who trusted me to explain concepts they couldn't yet grasp on their own.

I started to understand that being a student and being a guide were not opposites. They were connected. The more I taught, the more I learned. The more I learned, the better I could teach. Growth didn't move in a straight line upward—it cycled deeper, then outward.

At that stage of my journey, I didn't yet know what kind of instructor I would one day become. But I did know this much: teaching wasn't something you earned only after mastering the path. Sometimes, teaching is what helps you begin mastering it at all.

No official title declared that I was becoming an instructor. I didn't suddenly wake up one day and feel like a leader. Teaching arrived gradually, woven into class routines, whispered through responsibilities assigned without much attention. I didn't introduce myself as someone who could guide others—one day, I simply realized people already saw me that way.

Even then, I didn't see myself as someone who had all the answers. I still considered myself a student first. But now, I was a student who had begun learning differently. I absorbed techniques not just with the intention of performing them correctly, but with the intention of carrying them clearly. I began listening to instructors more critically—not in doubt, but with purpose, almost asking silently, *How would I explain this to someone else?*

My mindset was changing, even if I hadn't put words to it yet. Without realizing it, I had stepped into a role that expected me to live what I taught, not just repeat what I had learned. That expectation didn't come with applause or enhanced recognition—it came with an internal shift, a deeper sense of purpose behind every repetition.

I didn't feel like I had mastered anything. In fact, teaching made me see how long the road ahead still was. But it also helped me recognize that the path wasn't just about building myself up—it was about eventually helping others find their footing along the way. I didn't know it then, but those early moments of guiding others were shaping the kind of martial artist—and eventually, the kind of instructor—I would grow into. Before I fully understood leadership, I was already being trained by it.

As I continued guiding others, even in small ways, I didn't realize that something foundational was already shifting inside me. I wasn't trying to become a leader, but teaching was slowly shaping me into one. I wasn't chasing authority—I was learning accountability. I wasn't trying to stand above anyone—I was trying not to let anyone fall behind.

There's a moment in every martial artist's journey when training stops being just about their own growth and starts becoming about what they represent to others. Even though I hadn't declared myself ready to lead, the role had already begun teaching me how to carry myself with more clarity, patience, and purpose. I didn't always feel prepared, but I began to feel responsible.

That responsibility didn't give me an inflated sense of importance—it grounded me. It reminded me that people don't follow belts, they follow consistency. They don't trust rank, they trust character. The deeper I grew in understanding, the more I felt that being an example wasn't about being flawless—it was about being faithful to the journey, even when it tested me.

At that stage of my life, I didn't yet know how many challenges would test that sense of responsibility. I didn't understand how much pressure could weigh on someone expected to be solid while navigating their own doubts. But I was beginning to sense that leadership wasn't something you claimed—it was something you grew into, often before you realized it was happening. Teaching didn't make me feel like I had arrived. It made me feel like I had just begun a different kind of journey.

One where people didn't just watch how fast I advanced—

They watched how I walked when the way became difficult.

TEACHING MEANT LEADING WITH THE MIND FIRST

As I continued helping students, I reached a point where teaching wasn't just about explaining movements anymore—it became about holding a certain kind of presence. There were days when I didn't feel mentally sharp or physically strong, when doubt would creep in or frustration lingered from my own training. But if I stepped in front of students during one of those days, I had to leave that uncertainty behind. They weren't just watching how I moved—they were watching how I carried myself.

It wasn't that I wanted to hide what I felt. It was that I understood something new: if I let my internal struggle spill into my teaching, it could shake the confidence of someone who was only just beginning to believe they were capable. Students often look at their instructor as a reference point not just for technique, but for how to respond when things get difficult. If I let my shoulders sag or frustration show, it didn't just reflect on me—it shaped how they believed they were allowed to react when challenged.

There were days I had to dig deeper than I expected, not to perform better, but to remain composed. That quiet composure didn't mean I wasn't struggling—it meant I refused to let my struggle distract someone else from their own progress. There's a unique kind of test in being expected to remain steady when internally you're questioning whether you're delivering enough. In those moments, I learned something important: leadership doesn't wait until you feel completely ready—it often demands presence even when you're still working through your own doubts.

Teaching before fully knowing taught me how to anchor myself not in certainty, but in calmness. I began to understand that guiding others didn't require me to be perfect—it required me to be present, steady, and willing to give everything I had in that moment, even when what I had didn't feel like much.

Sometimes, strength wasn't about hitting harder or moving faster— it was about not letting internal noise shake the confidence of those who were still trying to find their rhythm.

Over time, holding steady under quiet pressure became a kind of training in itself—one that wasn't part of any curriculum, yet shaped me more deeply than many physical drills. Remaining composed while instructing others, even when I felt uncertain inside, taught me how to separate momentary emotion from long-term purpose. It forced me to understand that feeling uncertain didn't mean I lacked ability—it meant I was still growing through responsibility.

Teaching became a lesson in emotional discipline. I had to learn to breathe through mental noise, choose clarity over hesitation, and stay patient even when students struggled repeatedly. I couldn't rush them just because I was tired. I couldn't let frustration set the tone of the room. The more I taught, the more I understood that leadership didn't come from being louder or more dominant—it came from being controlled, calm, and consistent.

Some days, I didn't feel like showing up with energy or patience—but I did anyway, not because I wanted to look strong, but because someone in that class might be looking for stability that day. That thought alone sharpened my commitment. It made me realize that presence wasn't just about being physically there—it was about being mentally attentive and emotionally stable, especially when others were still trying to find their own center.

I didn't know it then, but these quiet moments of holding internal pressure without showing it were preparing me for far more intense moments down the road. Before I ever stepped into competitions that would test my mind more than my body, before I pushed through injury or stepped into environments where fear and pain were real, I was already being trained for it—here, in these early moments where I had to stay composed not for myself, but for others.

Teaching forced me to become emotionally stronger before I ever realized that mental resilience would one day become one of my greatest weapons.

As I continued teaching through moments of internal discomfort, I started noticing something about myself: even when my body wasn't at its strongest, my ability to stay mentally present allowed me to guide others effectively. That realization changed the way I viewed strength. Physical capability was important—but it wasn't always what people needed from me in those moments. Sometimes, what they needed most was my focus.

In time, I began to understand that every technique began in the mind before it was executed by the body. When a student hesitated, it wasn't because their legs couldn't kick or their arms couldn't strike—it was because something in their mind hadn't yet fully committed to the motion. Teaching required me to see hesitation not just as a physical flaw, but as an internal barrier.

The more I guided others, the more I learned to anticipate where a student's confidence would falter. I had to speak to their mindset before correcting their posture. I found myself saying things like, "Commit to the motion," or "Don't doubt yourself halfway through." At first, I said those things for their sake—but before long, I realized I was saying them for my own as well.

Teaching required mental clarity, not just technical accuracy. And that demand started reshaping the way I trained. Instead of simply repeating movements until they became familiar, I began controlling my breathing, steadying my thoughts, and setting my intention *before* moving. I practiced being composed so I could stay composed—even when my body or emotions tried to shift me off balance.

Without realizing it, teaching had led me to one of the most important breakthroughs in my martial arts journey: true control begins in the mind before it ever reaches the body.

Everything I believed about strength was slowly shifting. And soon, I would be tested in moments where technique alone wouldn't be enough.

Looking back, I didn't realize at the time just how much those early teaching moments were preparing me for the challenges ahead. I thought I was simply helping others grow—but in reality, I was being shaped just as much through the process. Staying composed while guiding students through their uncertainty taught me to steady myself even when I wasn't fully confident. Finding words that unlocked their understanding helped clarify my own. Leading with calmness when they hesitated taught me to face my own internal hesitation with focus, not fear.

What I didn't know then was that one day I would face moments where I couldn't rely on comfort, familiarity, or physical certainty. There would be times when my body would be exhausted, injured, or pushed to its limits. And in those moments, I wouldn't be able to rely on strength alone. I would need the mental discipline I had unknowingly built in those quiet teaching sessions—the discipline to breathe through doubt, maintain clarity in discomfort, and move forward with purpose even when part of me wanted to step back.

Teaching didn't make me invincible—it made me intentional. It didn't remove fear or struggle—it taught me how to carry them with calmness instead of panic. And when the time came for tests that went beyond explaining basics or holding posture under watchful eyes, I would draw from the same lessons I had given others:

Stay composed.
Stay clear.
Lead with your mind before your body follows.

I didn't fully understand it yet, but the path ahead would demand exactly that. And soon, I would begin to learn that physical strength alone couldn't carry me through what was coming next.

WINNING IN THE MIND BEFORE MOVING THE BODY

When I stepped into sparring sessions as a higher-ranked martial artist, something felt different. It wasn't just another round of training—it carried a quiet expectation. Students didn't just want instruction anymore; they wanted to test what instruction looked like in motion. They wanted to see if what I taught held up when things moved faster, hit harder, and pressed into instinct.

I didn't enter those matches trying to dominate or prove I was untouchable—teaching had already sharpened my understanding beyond ego. But I also didn't want to lose casually or appear unsteady. It wasn't pride—it was responsibility. If I set a standard for composure and clarity,

I needed to uphold it even when someone was trying to break through my guard.

Sparring became less about winning or losing and more about maintaining balance—for myself and for the students I was helping develop. I wasn't there to shut someone down or overwhelm them. I was there to give them something real to push against, something that made them adjust, think, and grow. At the same time, I had to remain sharp enough to show that experience mattered—not because it made me unbeatable, but because it made me controlled.

Losing wasn't my greatest fear—but losing my composure was. I didn't want a moment of frustration or recklessness to teach the wrong lesson. My goal wasn't to break the spirit of someone learning how to press forward—it was to challenge them without abandoning calm. If I let panic or ego enter the match, I wasn't just failing myself—I was failing the role I had slowly grown into.

In those rounds, I learned that sparring wasn't about seeing who walked away looking stronger. It was about whether I could remain composed, measured, and intentional—even when speed increased and contact landed harder than expected. I had to hold the standard without crushing the progression of those rising toward it.

On the surface, sparring tested physical ability. But internally, it tested everything I had learned about presence, patience, and purpose.

As time went on, sparring brought a new kind of energy to the floor—not just for me, but for those I trained with. Some students entered rounds with me quietly focused, wanting to improve. Others stepped forward with a different fire in their eyes. They didn't just want to train—they wanted to see where they stood in comparison to me.

There's a point in every martial artist's journey where someone begins to look at you as a benchmark. For some, that means pushing themselves to keep up. For others, it becomes an attempt to prove something—sometimes to themselves, sometimes to everyone watching. When I realized I had become that benchmark for certain students, the pressure shifted again. Every round wasn't just about technical execution—it was about setting the right tone even when someone else was trying to force the pace.

Some students would come at me harder, faster, hoping to catch me off guard. I could feel their urgency—an invisible question pulsing through each exchange: *Can I beat him?* I understood that desire. I had once been that student, looking for signs that I was progressing by testing myself against someone further down the path. So I didn't resent it—but I also couldn't allow their energy to drag me into reckless rhythms.

Meeting force with force would have only taught them that aggression wins. Overwhelming them too harshly would have discouraged growth. Letting them break through my defense without challenge would have sent the wrong message entirely. The balance was delicate: give them work, let them push, but hold the standard firmly with calm precision.

Those rounds reminded me that sparring wasn't always about being tested physically—it was about being tested mentally. Could I control the pace? Could I absorb intensity without escalating it? Could I allow room for challenge while still showing what disciplined response looked like?

In many ways, I realized that staying composed against someone desperate to prove themselves was a lesson I had to give more by example than by words. And sometimes, the most powerful statement wasn't delivering the hardest strike, but showing them that even their strongest attempts couldn't shake my control.

As the intensity of sparring increased, I began to notice a pattern. The students who rushed in aggressively often lost control not because they lacked strength or speed, but because they let emotion lead their movement. Their breathing would quicken. Their strikes would tighten. Their reactions became more reactive than intentional.

That's when I began to understand that sparring wasn't simply about trading technique—it was about *controlling rhythm, reading mindset, and staying calm when someone else was trying to create chaos.* If I stayed composed, I could see openings more clearly. If I breathed with intention, I could conserve energy while others burned through theirs quickly. The match was decided in the mind long before it showed in the body.

There were rounds where I felt physically pushed, where my legs were burning and my guard grew heavy—but as long as my mind stayed clear, I could regain control. When an opponent pressed forward recklessly, I didn't need to overpower them—I only needed to let their energy create its own vulnerability. Many times, I found that a well-timed counter or a controlled redirection broke their confidence more than any heavy strike could have.

The more I applied this, the more I understood that mental composure wasn't just part of sparring—it was the foundation of it. In training, we spent countless hours drilling movements, sharpening reflexes, and conditioning the body. But none of that mattered if the mind panicked. Without mental clarity, strength became sloppy, speed became reckless, and skill fell apart under pressure.

Teaching had forced me to think clearly while explaining. Sparring now demanded that I think clearly while under fire. Both were forms of leadership—one verbal, one physical—but both required the same internal anchor: stay present, stay calm, stay intentional.

In these moments, I realized something I would carry with me long beyond the sparring floor:

You don't win because you throw first. You win because you think before the other person loses control.

Sparring became more than a physical test—it revealed what happened when pressure collided with expectation. Every round wasn't about showing dominance or remaining untouchable; it was about demonstrating that control could exist even in motion, even under strike, even when others tried to break rhythm through force. In those moments, the lessons I had learned through teaching began to stabilize me in real time.

When I had helped students work through frustration, I didn't realize I was rehearsing for moments when I would have to calm myself in the middle of a match. When I learned to breathe slowly while explaining techniques, I didn't yet know that same kind of breathing would keep me from burning out when an opponent tried to overwhelm me. When I practiced explaining "why" a stance mattered, I didn't realize I was building internal trust in the structure I relied on when I needed to hold my ground.

These weren't things written in manuals or called out during training—they were realizations layered quietly over time. And it wasn't until those sparring sessions, under the eyes of those who looked to me as a standard, that I truly saw how much my mind mattered in every exchange.

There came a moment when I understood something important: Anyone can fight when they feel strong.
But a martial artist must be able to fight when they don't.

That meant sparring wasn't just conditioning my body—it was conditioning my response to discomfort, doubt, fatigue, and the pressure of expectation. It wasn't preparing me for the next match—it was preparing me for the moments in life when resistance wouldn't wait for me to feel ready.

The deeper I went into martial arts, the more I realized that strength without discipline could become reckless, and discipline without mindset could crumble under fear or exhaustion. Teaching taught me clarity. Sparring taught me control. But both experiences pointed me toward a greater truth that I didn't fully understand yet:

There comes a time when muscle alone isn't enough—when the fight shifts inside the mind before it ever expresses itself through the body.

I didn't know it yet, but I was heading toward that next lesson.

CHAPTER IV

Mind Over Muscle

◆

Ages before I ever faced a crucible moment, I began noticing something discomforting during sparring rounds and classes. Some people were already defeated before they even touched gloves. Their demeanor gave it away. Shoulders slightly tensed. Breathing heavy. Eyes wandering instead of staying focused. They stepped forward physically, but mentally, they were already taking steps back.

I saw fighters with strength, speed, and technique break simply because their mind had already surrendered to fear or doubt. A powerful kick thrown without conviction landed weaker than a slower one delivered with certainty. A stance formed from panic broke down faster than one held through stillness. It wasn't always the stronger fighter who won—it was often the one who stayed composed. That realization stayed with me:

The mind doesn't just influence the fight—it often determines it before it begins.

I started wondering...*What causes someone to lose before being hit?* Is it fear of pain? Shame of losing in front of others? Visualizing their opponent overpowering them before it happens in reality? I didn't have all the answers, but I had seen enough to know this:

Whoever controls their mind first controls the match, even before the bodies make contact.

This was more than physical training—it was a lesson in how belief shapes outcome. As I watched others fold under imagined pressure, I quietly asked myself:

What would I do when fear tried to get there before I did?
Would I step into the ring ready to fight... or already halfway lost?

I didn't know it yet, but I was asking the right questions.
The real test was still coming.

EARNING MY PLACE AMONG BLACK BELTS

The first real test of mental endurance didn't come from an opponent in a tournament—it came from standing among those who were supposed to be my peers.

When my father created an all–black belt class that brought together Karatekas from multiple schools he led, it wasn't just a showcase of skill—it was a silent measuring ground. I was one of the youngest in that room, surrounded by older, larger, stronger martial artists who had worn their belts longer than I had even been training at their level.

No one said it out loud, but there was an unspoken tension in the space:

You might be wearing the same belt... but have you earned it the same way we did?

Standing there, I wasn't just aware of my youth—I was aware of every expectation I imagined others might have. I could feel that this wasn't about executing techniques; nevertheless, it was about proving, without words, that I belonged in that lineup. Every drill, every stance, every strike carried an invisible weight—not of performance, but of credibility.

It wasn't fear of being hit that got to me. It was the fear of not living up to what the belt around my waist claimed I was. That quiet voice that whispered, *"You're younger… smaller… do they believe you belong here?"* began testing me the moment we bowed in. But here's what shifted:

As training intensified, and sweat set in, I realized that I didn't need to be the strongest or fastest in the room.

What mattered more was how I responded when the pace increased, when the drills demanded endurance, when fatigue tried to break form.

I didn't have to win against anyone—
I just couldn't let myself mentally break in front of them.

Holding my stance when others were watching became its own kind of victory. Keeping my breathing steady when rounds went long became proof—not to them, but to myself—that I could hold my place. I wasn't trying to outperform them—I was trying not to let intimidation dictate how I moved. That class didn't teach me new techniques. It taught me a deeper truth:

Sometimes, the first opponent you have to defeat is the version of yourself that questions if you belong in the arena at all.

THE WOMAN WHO ABSORBED STRIKES

During the camps my father hosted, students from across the country came to train for the weekend. It wasn't just a test of endurance—it was exposure. New styles, new rhythms, new expectations. And among the instructors brought in to teach, some were from different parts of the world, carrying influences and intensity we weren't always used to.

Those camps weren't about belts. They were about finding out how you responded outside your comfort zone—surrounded by strangers, among black belts with different lineages, under instructors who pushed you until you either adapted or broke.

But there was one moment that stayed with me more than any drill, kata, or technique we practiced.

One of my father's instructors—a woman whose presence was quiet but undeniably strong—stood in a ring formed by students. Several strong, capable martial artists were invited to strike her midsection with power. No blocking. No bracing theatrically. Just receiving the blow.

And they hit her hard. Not with hesitation, but with the kind of force meant to prove something.

She didn't flinch.

Not a waver in her stance.

Not a change in her eyes.

Not even the slightest exhale of pain or resistance.

It wasn't that the strikes didn't land. It was that they couldn't move her—not because her body was unbreakable, but because *her mind was unshakable*.

Watching her absorb each hit with complete composure, I realized something important:

She wasn't fighting their strikes—she was outlasting them with stillness.

She didn't need to show power. She *was* power, because she showed no need to react. That moment shifted something in me. I began to ask myself:

Is strength always about force… or sometimes about unshakeable calm?
Can the strongest fighter be the one who refuses to be moved mentally, even when struck physically?

Is it possible that mastery isn't about having no weaknesses—but about having control so deep that no one else can dictate your reactions?

Suddenly, toughness wasn't just about impact. It was about presence under impact. She didn't just teach that day with words—She taught with stillness. And that image stayed with me long after the camp ended. It made me wonder, *If someone could remain that composed under force… what could I do if I trusted my mind with that same conviction?*

That question would follow me into the ring of a regional tournament—Where I would face an opponent whose presence alone tested my mindset before the first strike was thrown.

FIGHTING THE OPPONENT BEFORE THE FIRST STRIKE

By the time I entered that regional tournament, I had already seen fear defeat people from the inside out. I had stood among black belts older and stronger than me and held my ground through quiet intimidation. I had witnessed resilience that didn't look loud or aggressive—but absolutely unbreakable.

But none of that meant the pressure wasn't real when I saw *him*. He was taller than most competitors there—long reach, explosive movement, and a presence that made people hesitate before stepping forward. I watched him fight earlier rounds, and every opponent he faced looked smaller, not because of size, but because of the way fear shrunk them. He didn't just fight them—he *loomed* over them. One by one, competitors fell to the same signature move: a powerful axe kick crashing down with speed and force that sent bodies stumbling back or falling to the floor.

Each time he landed it, the room reacted. Some in awe. Some in concern. Some in dread, wondering who might be next.

When he finished his match before mine, there was a sudden stillness—like people knew he would be advancing, and they were already thinking ahead. I could feel eyes shift toward me. Maybe they wanted to know how I would react. Maybe they wondered if I would fold like the others.

But before I stepped into the ring, I felt something steadying me from within—not defiance, not arrogance, but clarity. The same clarity I had seen in that instructor absorbing strikes without reacting. The same stillness I had held onto when surrounded by seasoned black belts. The same awareness I felt when I understood that fear only held the power we gave it.

My brother looked at me—no words, just a look that said he knew I was ready. Not because I was stronger than the opponent—but because I was *calm*.

As I prepared to face him, I didn't focus on his size or power. Instead, I replayed what I had seen—especially that axe kick. I pictured it in slow motion, visualizing where I would be, how I would counter, how I would control the exchange before it spiraled into chaos.

So when the referee shouted *"Hajime"*, I wasn't just reacting—I was already acting from a place of mental control.

He launched his axe kick just as expected.

But this time, I wasn't one of the competitors already defeated by it.

I stepped into my visualization, caught his leg mid-air, and unleashed sharp, controlled strikes to his body. His balance broke. His presence shattered. The arena that had once echoed with surprise at his dominance now reacted with shock as he hit the floor.

In that moment—right there, mid-match—I didn't roar in celebration or fuel myself with adrenaline. I simply exhaled, deeply and calmly. Because that was the moment I knew:

My body was following a mind that refused to be intimidated.

I stayed composed for the rest of the fight—not rushing, not overreaching, not letting excitement turn into recklessness. The match ended with me winning not because I was the fastest or strongest—but because I stayed *clear.*

That day, I didn't just win a regional tournament. I proved to myself that fear is only as strong as your willingness to let it dictate your movements.

THE FIGHT WAS WON BEFORE I STEPPED ONTO THE FLOOR

After the match ended, I didn't feel the explosive rush some fighters chase. I didn't feel like I had conquered someone—I felt like I had confirmed something. The real win happened long before my arm was raised. It happened before the first strike, before the referee called us in, before I bowed.

It happened the moment I refused to let intimidation control my breathing.

The fight with that opponent wasn't about strength versus strength—it was about belief versus doubt. He had used fear as his first weapon, and many had fallen to it without realizing they surrendered before they even touched him. But I had learned to prepare my mind to meet him before my body did.

In that fight, I realized something that would stick with me throughout my martial arts journey:

Your opponent is not always the person standing across from you. Sometimes, your opponent is the version of yourself that hesitates under pressure.

And when you defeat that version, everything after becomes clearer, calmer, more controlled.

I didn't leave that match thinking I was unbeatable. I left it knowing something far more important: I now understood what it meant to *trust my mental readiness more than my physical instinct.*

That wasn't the end of my journey with fear or pressure. There would be harder challenges ahead, moments where pain cut through calm, where exhaustion blurred my judgment, and where injury would test my resilience in a way physical strength alone could not carry.

But now I had a new compass. I started to train my mindset with intention—visualizing under pressure, breathing through tension, learning to stay composed even when discomfort crept in. Because from that day forward, I knew this:

A strong body helps you fight.
A strong mind helps you endure.
But a disciplined mind helps you win long before the match even begins.

PREPARING FOR STORMS YET TO COME

That regional tournament didn't make me fearless—but it proved that fear didn't have to lead me. It showed me that strength wasn't about overpowering others, but about mastering my own reactions. It taught me that clarity under pressure is earned long before contact is made.

From that moment on, I began to train differently.

Not harder—*smarter.*

Not recklessly—*intentionally.*

Not just to perform—but to stay composed no matter what I faced.

I practiced breathing through fatigue. I visualized opponents stronger, faster, more aggressive than me—not to scare myself, but to prepare my mind to stay calm when the moment arrived. I trained not just to throw harder strikes, but to keep my mind steady in moments when panic would tempt me to rush or retreat.

I didn't know it then, but that clarity would become crucial later, when the challenges ahead weren't just about facing a stronger fighter— but about pushing through pain, injury, and moments where the body wanted to quit long before the soul was ready to surrender.

That tournament taught me how to step into fear without letting it break my rhythm. But life and training had much bigger tests waiting— where I would face internal battles far deeper than intimidation.

Soon, I would learn there are moments when technique fails, when physical strength fades, and when even confidence wavers. And in those moments, only one question remains:

Will your mind push forward, or give in?

"Brotherhood is not formed by standing together,
but by refusing to let each other fall."

CHAPTER V

Brotherhood

People often talk about martial arts as a personal journey—a path walked alone, disciplined by one's own willpower and desire to improve. And in many ways, that's true. No one can throw a strike for you. No one can stand in your stance, breathe through your lungs, or push past fatigue inside your body.

But there's something different about growing up on the mats beside someone who refuses to let you stay where you are—not through speeches or motivation—but through their presence alone.

For me, that someone was my brother.

He was older, stronger, and always just one step ahead. He never told me to work harder or asked if I could keep up. He didn't have to. Just showing up to train next to him demanded that I push forward or fall behind. There were no verbal challenges, no dramatic calls to greatness. We didn't hype each other up or talk about winning. We just trained—and in that silence, standards were set.

In those early years, I didn't see him as competition in a loud, ego-driven way. I saw him as the pace-setter—the marker of where I needed to be if I wanted to be worthy of calling myself his equal. And I didn't want to just follow him—I wanted to stand beside him without feeling like I was lesser.

One training day stands out clearly in my memory. We were going at it hard, later in our childhood but before we were fully grown. The intensity between brothers is different. You don't pull back when you're family—if anything, you push each other harder because there's trust beneath the impact.

In one of those exchanges, he landed a well-timed kick that caught me square and hard enough to knock me backward—straight through a drywall panel.

He didn't stop to apologize. I didn't sit there to consider whether it was too much. We didn't talk about it or question whether we had gone too far. The moment wasn't defined by the kick—it was defined by what came next.

I stood up and stepped right back in front of him.

Not with anger. Not with tears. Not with fear.

Just with resolve.

And he didn't ease up.

In that exchange, we didn't say a single word—but something important was spoken. He wasn't testing whether he could hit me—I was testing whether I would still stand after being hit. That moment didn't teach me to be tougher because of pain—it revealed that I was willing to keep going, even when my body was rattled. Looking back, I realize that was one of the first times I understood something important:

Brotherhood in martial arts isn't about encouragement—it's about pressure that comes from someone who trusts you to rise.

He never had to tell me I was capable. He fought me like I was. And in doing so, he gave me a choice—to either meet the intensity or back down.

I chose to meet it.

That was the beginning of realizing that martial arts may be an individual journey—but some parts of you are only discovered when someone else refuses to slow down just so you can catch your breath.

SILENT RIVALRY, LOUD GROWTH

Training beside someone you respect is different than training beside a stranger. With others, you can pace yourself, pull back when tired, or hide moments of doubt. But when you train next to someone you've grown up with—someone who has seen you tired, frustrated, unfocused, or unsure—you can't hide. And when that person never gives you an easy round, you learn very quickly that effort has to meet effort. That was the quiet rivalry my brother and I shared.

We didn't call each other out.

We didn't trash talk.

We never said, *"Let's see who does this better."*

We simply trained.

But there was always a silent understanding: *if one of us pushed harder, the other would match it.* No one wanted to be the one who eased up first. No one wanted to look like they were fading while the other remained steady.

This wasn't a rivalry built on jealousy or pride—it was built on mutual respect. When my brother pushed the pace, I didn't think, *He's trying to beat me.* I thought, *He's showing what's possible… now I have to decide if I'm willing to go there too.*

And when I pushed back in later years, I wasn't trying to dethrone him—I was proving that everything he poured into his training had ignited something powerful in me, too.

Our sparring rounds were never casual. Even when we weren't trying to hurt each other, we were always trying to test each other. Not to see who was better—but to see who could remain composed longer, strike cleaner, recover faster, adapt more intelligently.

Some rounds were intense and fast. Some were slow and strategic. But every one of them said something, even if no words were spoken.

When one of us landed a clean strike, we didn't celebrate—we recalibrated. When someone faltered for a moment, the other didn't slow down—they pressed in, because we both understood that learning to recover under pressure mattered more than avoiding discomfort.

We didn't train for each other.

We trained because of each other.

That rivalry didn't create distance—it created growth. And eventually, it laid the foundation for something even stronger: balance. There came a point where neither of us was clearly chasing the other anymore. We were running the same race—just on parallel lanes, pushing each other forward without ever needing to say a word.

BROTHERHOOD IN VICTORY AND DEFEAT

When you grow up training beside someone who pushes you, competition doesn't disappear—it just matures. There were times when my brother progressed faster than me in certain techniques or looked sharper in drills. There were moments he seemed more fluid during sparring or absorbed feedback more efficiently. In those times, I had to make a choice: see his progress as a threat—or as proof that growth was still possible for me.

I chose the second.

Watching him improve didn't discourage me; it confirmed that there was still room for me to rise. When he landed cleaner strikes, it didn't make me feel small—it reminded me where I needed to adjust. When he adapted faster, I didn't see it as him pulling away—I saw it as him reminding me to evolve.

And in return, my growth did the same for him.

There were days when I found a rhythm he hadn't yet locked into. Times when I executed a technique with more precision or applied a new concept more efficiently. When that happened, he didn't tear me down or treat it like a loss. He pushed forward, let it drive him, and sharpened himself further. We didn't fight to stay above each other—we fought to keep the standard high.

That's the difference between rivalry and brotherhood: In rivalry, victory is about being above the other person.In brotherhood, victory is when both of you rise—sometimes one after the other—without losing respect in the process.

Even when one of us had the upper hand in a particular round or drill, it wasn't a finish line. It was a cue. A signal. A reminder that excellence wasn't a moment—it was a rhythm we had to maintain.

Wins didn't create distance between us. They created motivation. Losses didn't cause resentment—they caused reflection. If one of us struggled, the other didn't soften—we pushed harder, knowing that protection doesn't always come from easing pressure. Sometimes, protection comes from holding your brother to the level you know he's capable of reaching.

Over time, the back-and-forth of who was "ahead" faded into something more balanced. We still pushed each other. We still trained with intensity. But it became less about who struck cleaner that day and more about who stayed committed for the long haul.

In the end, brotherhood wasn't about winning or losing against each other. It was about not letting each other stay less than what we could be.

THE ONE YOU TRUST TO EXPOSE WEAKNESS

Training with strangers tests your reaction time.
Training with instructors tests your discipline.
But training with someone who knows you—your habits, your flaws, your patterns—tests your truth.

Over time, my brother became more than someone I pushed myself against—he became someone I trusted to push me when I began to plateau. We had trained beside each other long enough for him to recognize the subtle signs when I was holding back or hesitating. He could see doubt in movements others might think were just slow reactions. He could tell when I was sparring with caution instead of conviction—not because he was analyzing me, but because he had walked the same mental roads himself.

With him, there was no hiding behind effort. If I gave 90%, he knew it. If I was stuck repeating a mistake, he noticed. And when he saw it, he didn't ease up—he pressured me in exactly the way I needed, not out of frustration, but out of belief that I could push further.

It wasn't spoken, but there was a quiet agreement built over countless rounds:

"I won't let you go easy on yourself—and I expect you won't let me, either."

In that trust, sparring changed meaning. We weren't just exchanging strikes—we were exchanging honesty. When he landed something clean, it wasn't meant to embarrass me; it was a reminder that I needed to adjust, refine, and respond. When I found a way through his guard, it wasn't a victory over him—it was a signal that something in our training was working.

There's a rare kind of confidence that comes from having someone who will strike you without hesitation—not out of malice, but because he believes you are capable of absorbing it, learning from it, and responding with growth.

He became the one I could fail in front of without losing pride—and succeed against without having to boast. When exhaustion hit, he knew whether it was physical fatigue or mental retreat—and he treated them differently. If my body was failing, he'd let me breathe. If my mind was failing, he'd keep the pressure on until I remembered how to fight through it.

That level of trust doesn't form overnight. It's forged through shared rounds, hard falls, quiet nods, and unspoken respect.

Eventually, I stopped training to catch up to him—and started training knowing he would never let me settle.

By the time we were older, the idea of "catching up" to my brother had faded. We weren't chasing each other anymore—we were moving forward together, sometimes one slightly ahead, sometimes the other, but always knowing that either way, we were stronger because the other existed.

Brotherhood wasn't just something that happened in sparring rounds—it became something woven into how I faced challenges outside the dojo. When I trained alone, I could still feel the silent standard he helped set. The same internal voice that drove me to get up after being dropped through drywall was the one that told me not to ease up when training pushed me into discomfort. Even when he wasn't in the room, the intensity of our shared sessions lived in my conditioning, in my focus, in my refusal to quit early.

There's a kind of strength that develops when you know someone out there understands exactly how hard you've pushed yourself—because they've pushed themselves the same way. It creates an invisible support system. Not verbal. Not visible. But undeniably real.

As we matured, our roles shifted naturally—not by rank or entitlement, but by need. At times, he led in intensity, and I followed. At other times, I grew in clarity or technical execution, and he allowed my focus to sharpen his. We didn't talk about it, label it, or point it out—it just happened. Strength passed between us like a steady, rhythmic breath. A constant exhale of challenge, followed by an inhale of growth.

Looking back, I realize that brotherhood didn't make the journey easier—it made it unavoidable. There was no space to fall behind when someone close to you was consistently stepping forward. Your only options were to match the movement—or admit to yourself that you chose to stop. And stopping never felt like an option when your example was looking straight at you, even in silence.

We weren't always equals in strength. We weren't always even in mentality. But over time, our growth became connected. We sharpened each other without asking to. We challenged each other without needing to. And when it truly mattered—when future tests came, whether physical, mental, or emotional—we both carried into those moments the quiet knowledge:

We never trained alone. And because of that, we grew into more than we would have on our own.

"Staying the same may feel safe—but growth demands movement, even when the direction is uncertain."

CHAPTER VI
Evolving Through the Art

♦

There's comfort in routine—especially when you grow up training in a place that feels like home. I knew the floor, the rhythm of drills, the way classes were structured. I knew the energy of the room, the familiar push of sparring, the unspoken expectations. And for a long time, that environment helped shape who I was.

But over time, something inside me quietly shifted.

It wasn't caused by doubt or dissatisfaction. It was something subtler—like an itch beneath the surface that I couldn't ignore. I didn't feel stagnant, but I began to wonder how much more there was beyond what I already knew. I had learned countless techniques, drilled thousands of repetitions, stood alongside people I respected—but a feeling lingered:

What would happen if I stepped outside everything I was comfortable with?

Life eventually made that decision for me when I moved away from home for several years. Suddenly, the place where I had always trained was no longer an option. My familiar training grounds, routines, and partners weren't there. I wasn't just outside my comfort zone—I had no idea where my new zone was supposed to be.

I could have taken that as a season to pause or to coast on what I already knew. Instead, being disconnected from my foundation forced me to search—to seek training environments I had never experienced before.

Walking into new dojos as a stranger felt strange after years of being rooted in familiarity. Here, no one knew my background, my belt rank, my story, or my family's martial legacy. I didn't step in as a seasoned practitioner—I stepped in as someone ready to learn again.

And in that unfamiliar space, I began to evolve in ways that staying home never would have allowed.

The farther I moved from what I knew, the closer I came to understanding what I could still become.

THE BOXER WHO CHANGED MY HANDS

During my time away from home, I met a professional boxer who had once challenged for the WBA Heavyweight Title—completely by chance. It didn't happen in a dojo or during training. It was just one of those unexpected moments life hands you before you understand how much it's going to shape you.

He didn't try to teach me in the traditional sense. He didn't lecture or correct or demonstrate. But through a few conversations, he shifted the way I understood striking. Up to that point, my punching came from structure—years of drilling, patterns, and repetition. Clean. Controlled. Familiar. But he wasn't just throwing punches. He was *reading* people. Dictating pace. Drawing reactions. Striking with intention that came from the mind long before it showed in the body.

He didn't talk about throwing hands—he talked about *owning space*.

He didn't talk about power—he talked about *clarity before movement*.

He didn't talk about hitting first—he talked about *making your opponent choose wrong*.

His language forced me to see striking differently—not as a sequence of techniques, but as an expression of timing, rhythm, and psychological presence. He didn't give me new tools. I could find those anywhere. He gave me *new perspective*. I stopped punching just to fill space and started striking with intent. I refined my jab so it meant something. I began to see exchanges as conversations—where intention, not motion, dictated direction.

What stayed with me most wasn't just his experience.
It was his calm.

The same steadiness I admired in the martial artists who raised me, I now saw through a boxer's lens. And in that moment, something clicked:

True evolution isn't about abandoning what you know—it's about letting new insight reshape how you apply it.

That encounter didn't turn me into a boxer.
It turned me into a martial artist who understood striking differently. I carried that insight with me into what came next, even before I understood how much it would matter.

A DOJO WITH MANY DOORS

The next step in my growth didn't come from mastering a single style—it came from walking into a dojo that didn't belong to just one.

The place I began training at didn't hold fast to one lineage or restrict itself to a single curriculum. Instead, it invited instructors from different backgrounds—Aikido, kickboxing, Dragon Kung-Fu, and other striking systems. Classes became less about repeating one school's way and more about being exposed to perspectives that challenged each other.

At first, it felt strange. I was used to structure—certain techniques executed a certain way because that's how they were taught, how they were meant to be preserved. But here, every session was a new question:

What if a strike enters this way? How does that affect your response? What happens when the rhythm changes? What if the opponent doesn't move the way you were trained to expect?

Suddenly, martial arts became fluid rather than fixed.

I saw the circular redirection of Aikido challenge the linear precision of boxing. I felt the explosiveness of kickboxing force adaptation in timing and defensive strategy. I noticed how some practitioners relied on aggression, others on patience, some on redirection, others on pressure.

There was no "right" way—only effective ways based on purpose, timing, and mindset.

This environment didn't force me to abandon what I knew—it forced me to examine it. Instead of blindly holding onto tradition, I began asking deeper questions:

- *Why does this technique work?*
- *When does it fail?*
- *What adjustments keep it alive across different styles?*
- *How do I adapt rather than clash against a different rhythm?*

The more perspectives I absorbed, the more I realized something:

There is strength in loyalty to a foundation—but there is mastery in understanding how that foundation moves under different conditions.

I didn't lose my original style—I evolved my relationship to it. And soon, I wasn't just learning techniques. I was learning to *flow*.

THE BIRTH OF MY OWN STYLE

As I continued training in this open environment, I didn't want to become someone who simply collected techniques from every style I encountered. I saw people try that—jumping from one system to another, mimicking everything they saw, but never fully embodying any of it. They moved like patchwork—pieces of everything, mastery of nothing. That wasn't what I wanted.

Every system I encountered had strengths, but they also had limitations based on timing, distance, body mechanics, or the opponent's mindset. Instead of copying full frameworks, I started to study *why* something worked, *when* it worked best, and *what it required mentally to use effectively.*

Slowly, I began fusing elements together—not by force, but through necessity. If a technique required sharper timing, I refined it with principles I'd learned from boxing. If a flow required smoother transitions, I remembered lessons from Aikido or redirection-based systems. If an exchange needed speed and pressure, I borrowed the intensity from kickboxing. But I didn't try to *become* those styles—I allowed them to refine me.

Rather than layering systems on top of each other, I allowed them to pass through me—letting my foundation absorb what aligned naturally with how I moved, thought, and responded.

It was no longer about fighting like anyone else. It was about fighting from a place of clarity rooted in everything I had learned, without abandoning who I already was.

This shift didn't just change how I fought.

It changed how I trained.

It changed how I taught.

I started to see that good instructors pass on knowledge.

But great instructors pass on *questions*—the kind that force students to explore and grow without becoming rigid copies of someone else. For the first time, I wasn't just practicing martial arts. I was *shaping my art.*

RETURNING AS A PRACTIONER WHO HAD CHANGED

When I eventually returned home, I didn't step back into the dojo as the same martial artist who had left. Leaving had stretched my perspective, forced adaptation, and challenged me to question deeply— not out of rebellion, but out of a desire to evolve with purpose. I wasn't returning with a new style—I was returning with a refined understanding of who I was within the art.

The martial world around me had changed, too. A new generation was rising—students inspired by cage fighting, MMA highlights, and the growing influence of Brazilian Jiu-Jitsu in modern combat sports. They didn't just want to train—they wanted to test themselves in different environments. They didn't want to only learn self-defense—they wanted to compete, adapt, and see how their skills held up under different pressures.

I saw this shift not as a threat to tradition, but as a call to evolve how we guided the next generation.

Instead of resisting change, I embraced it. I began incorporating elements I had learned from boxing, from kickboxing, from redirection-based movement, and from strategic striking philosophy. I worked with instructors in Brazilian Jiu-Jitsu to expand our ground game and introduced structures that allowed students to explore different ranges and transitions without abandoning core fundamentals.

I wasn't trying to replace what my family had built—I was strengthening it for what lay ahead.

Our roots remained our identity—but the branches began to reach further than before.

As I adjusted my teaching, I didn't force others to move like me. I encouraged them to understand why a technique works, how it transfers under different styles, and when to adapt rather than resist. I didn't tell them what to believe—I showed them how to think. Returning home, I realized something powerful:

My journey away wasn't a detour. It was preparation to return with clarity, conviction, and something meaningful to contribute.

The dojo became more than a place where I trained—it became a place where I helped others evolve in ways I once had to find on my own.

FIGHTERS REACT. MARTIAL ARTISTS RESPOND

As I continued training in new environments, one thing became increasingly clear: not everyone approached martial arts with the same intent. I came across many "fighters"—people who trained hard, hit hard, and entered every exchange like it was a personal challenge to prove dominance. Their energy was explosive, fast, fueled by adrenaline and emotion. They were quick, aggressive, and dangerous when charging forward. But I also noticed something: many of them reacted, not responded.

When their opponent moved, they chased.

When they were struck, they swung harder out of anger.

When pressured, they either rushed forward recklessly or broke under emotional strain.

Their movement was fueled by emotion, not guided by intention.

Their goal was often to overpower—not to outthink.

In contrast, I began intentionally shaping myself more firmly in the path of the martial artist. That didn't mean I rejected intensity—far from it. But I wanted every strike to have purpose, not just power. I wanted to maintain clarity under pressure, not swing out of panic. I wanted to adapt based on rhythm, distance, and mindset—not ego.

A fighter often asks, *"How do I hit harder?"*

A martial artist asks, *"How do I choose the right moment to hit—and why?"*

A fighter reacts when emotion spikes.

A martial artist responds when clarity leads.

Over time, I learned that the difference between reacting and responding is the difference between impulse and intention. That philosophy shaped everything—how I moved, how I adapted, how I trained, how I eventually began teaching again. And it became especially important when dealing with students who carried ego into the dojo. They weren't just learning techniques—they were fighting identity battles.

Some came in trying to prove something. Others tried to impose dominance.

Guiding them required more than physical instruction—it required responding rather than reacting. I couldn't meet their ego with ego. I had to meet their intensity with purpose. Teaching reminded me again:

Reaction is emotional.
Response is intentional.
One comes from fear or pride.
The other comes from understanding.

I knew which one I wanted to embody—and which one I hoped to pass on.

TESTED BY WHAT COMES NEXT

As I evolved, I became more settled in who I was—not just as someone who trained, but as someone who moved with intention. I had learned to adapt, to absorb new perspectives without losing my roots, to refine rather than abandon, and to guide others toward clarity instead of chaos.

I began to trust my ability to stay calm. To respond instead of react. To remain composed even when intensity rose. I had seen how exposure to different styles could refine me and how ego-driven fighters often burned out faster than practitioners who stayed grounded.

But evolution has a way of testing whether your philosophy is something you believe in... or something you've merely spoken enough times to feel comfortable with.

There comes a moment in every martial artist's journey when concepts can no longer stay in theory. When controlled environments are stripped away. When your body refuses to move the way it used to. When pain interrupts rhythm and fear is no longer theoretical. When movement—something once taken for granted—suddenly must be fought for. The true test of a belief is not when it's preached—it's when it's threatened.

I didn't know it at the time, but soon, I would face a moment where strength wouldn't look like holding perfect form, or landing clean strikes, or staying ahead of an opponent. It wouldn't be about adapting to someone else's rhythm, but to a broken rhythm inside my own body. And in that season, I would find out:

Can you still respond when your body wants to react?
Can you stay composed when pain clouds clarity?
Can you still evolve when movement feels like it's slipping away?

Injury was waiting—not as an ending, but as a new threshold. Everything I had learned so far had built me into someone who could move with purpose.

Soon, I would learn whether that purpose could endure when movement was taken away.

"A black belt carries a responsibility greater than technique: the responsibility to behave as someone worthy of wearing it."

CHAPTER VII

The Responsibility of the Black Belt

✦

Earning a black belt is often celebrated as the pinnacle of a martial artist's journey. People outside the art see it as a symbol of mastery. Even students who are early in their training sometimes treat it like a finish line. But the most surprising shift happens not in the belt itself—but in how others look at you once you wear it.

I earned my black belt young. It didn't make me feel invincible or superior, but I quickly realized it made people view me differently. Suddenly, students—some my age, some older—watched my technique a little more closely during drills. When an instructor demonstrated something, they glanced at me afterward to see how I executed it. There were no formal announcements that I was now an example—but my presence started being treated like one.

I noticed something else: some students disappeared after earning their black belt, as if reaching that rank marked the end of their journey. The ones who stayed gained a kind of quiet credibility—not just because we wore the belt, but because we continued to show up, sweat, fail, grow, and improve long after we could have walked away with a title. Over time, those who remained became the ones others looked to when they weren't sure how to move or how they were expected to carry themselves.

It wasn't that I tried to be a leader or that I demanded respect—it was that I stayed when others didn't.

With that consistency came shifts in responsibility. I was asked more often to demonstrate techniques. When younger or newer students paired off, instructors would position them near me, trusting I could guide without controlling, lead without overpowering. Teaching wasn't always official—but influence doesn't wait for permission. It happens the moment people start learning through your example.

That was when I first realized: a black belt doesn't just tell others what rank you've reached. It tells them what standard they expect you to hold.

At first, there was a subtle tension—balancing the humility of still being a student with the expectation from others that I already had the answers. But even then, something inside me understood: the belt wasn't permission to stop learning. It was permission to carry the weight of becoming someone others might follow.

That weight didn't crush me—but I could feel that it was there now.

And I knew I had to be someone who didn't let it slip from my shoulders.

TEACHING WITH AUTHORITY VS. TEACHING WITH INTEGRITY

As I began helping others more often—whether formally assisting or simply being the person students naturally watched—I noticed something subtle but important: people assumed that a black belt meant certainty. That every question had an answer. That every technique was already mastered. That mistakes were behind me.

But being given responsibility didn't suddenly erase my own doubts or areas where I was still growing. I was still figuring things out. I was still refining my form. I still made mistakes—sometimes big ones. There were nights I questioned whether I was explaining a movement clearly or just repeating something I had memorized long ago. And there were moments when I worried about being asked something I couldn't yet articulate well enough to teach. That's where a quiet choice had to be made:

Would I teach from a place of authority—or from a place of integrity?

Teaching from authority would have been easy—say things with confidence even when I wasn't fully confident myself. Give definitive answers simply because students expected them. Present myself as finished because the belt implied completion.

But that path felt wrong.

So, I chose integrity. If I knew something deeply, I explained it. If I understood it but was still refining it, I shared both my knowledge and my learning process. And if someone asked a question I couldn't yet answer fully, I didn't fake it. I said we'd break it down together, ask a higher-ranked instructor, or explore it more in the next session. That didn't make me weaker—it made me trustworthy. Over time, I learned something important:

Students don't connect to instructors who pretend to be perfect.
They connect to instructors who are honest in the process of becoming better.

Teaching forced me to deepen what I thought I already knew. When students asked *why* a technique worked a certain way, I couldn't just demonstrate it—I had to understand it. Their questions made me study deeper, think more critically, and perform more consistently. Teaching became one of the greatest tools in my own evolution—not because it made me look like a leader, but because it made me train like one.

A black belt doesn't guarantee flawless execution. It requires honest development. And teaching with humility didn't lessen my authority—it strengthened its foundation.

Over time, I realized that leadership in martial arts isn't about being the loudest voice or the one with all the answers. It's about being someone who refuses to stop learning—even while being watched.

HOLDING STANDARDS WHEN NO ONE IS WATCHING

As time went on, I began to understand something deeper about what it meant to be a black belt: it wasn't just about what people saw from me in class. It was about how I carried myself when no one was paying attention.

Inside the dojo, it was easy to be focused. Surrounded by other martial artists, drills, structure, and discipline, the environment itself pushed me to train with purpose. But outside, in everyday life—where there was no instructor watching, no uniform symbolizing intent, no students scanning for guidance—that's when the true test of internal discipline began. Being a black belt didn't just ask me to move better. It asked me to *live better.*

I started becoming more aware of how I responded to frustration, conflict, or disrespect. Was I reacting like someone who needed to win every encounter—or responding like someone who had learned control? When I didn't feel like training, did I still show up with consistency, or did I justify slipping because no one would know? When conversations turned negative or destructive, did I add fuel—or redirect the energy like I would redirect an aggressive strike?

I realized that martial arts doesn't just train your body to follow commands. It trains your character when comfort tempts you to drift.

Over time, I began to see a difference between those who wore a black belt and those who *lived as one.* Earning rank is an event—but maintaining its meaning is a decision made daily. It's not about pretending to be flawless. It's about holding a standard high enough that even when you fall short, you fall forward.

The belt around my waist no longer felt like just a symbol—it felt like a reminder.
A reminder that I wasn't just training for myself anymore.

A reminder that people—students, peers, even strangers—read character faster than they read skill.

A reminder that martial arts doesn't stop when the class ends.
A reminder that strength without responsibility becomes ego.

And so, even outside the dojo, I found myself walking a little more composed, breathing a little more intentionally, choosing patience over aggression—not to appear disciplined, but to remain aligned with who I was becoming.

The mat teaches you how to stand.
Life tests whether you'll stand the same when you step off of it.

DOJO EGO: GUIDE THE FIGHTER WITHOUT CRUSHING THEM

With time, a new responsibility began to surface—dealing with students who came in not to learn, but to prove something.

Some arrived already calling themselves fighters. They carried themselves with intensity and walked into sparring rounds like every exchange was a chance to dominate. You could see it in their eyes—the mindset of reacting out of pride rather than responding with discipline. Some swung too hard when it wasn't necessary. Others measured their worth only by whether they won the round. Their movements were fast, aggressive, fueled by emotion—and often unstable.

As a black belt, I had to decide what role I would play in their journey. I could have crushed them to prove hierarchy. I could have exposed their ego by overwhelming them. But that kind of victory doesn't teach—it only embarrasses. And embarrassment doesn't create better martial artists. It creates resentment and people who either quit or try to fight harder for reasons beyond purpose. So instead of destroying their confidence, I aimed to redirect their mindset.

When sparring with them, I didn't meet emotion with emotion. I stayed calm and precise—not to show superiority, but to let them feel the difference between reacting and responding. I didn't rush exchanges. I didn't trade blow for blow. I would intercept their aggression quietly, control the pace, and show that effectiveness wasn't about rage—it was about rhythm, clarity, and understanding.

I didn't need to say much. Most of the time, the lesson clicked without a lecture. They'd feel their energy burn out quickly while my breathing remained steady. They'd throw everything they had and still find themselves out-positioned—not because they were weak, but because raw power without purpose has limits. At times, after sparring, I'd offer small guidance—not in the form of criticism, but as questions:

- "What did you see just before you rushed in?"
- "What made you throw that punch right there?"
- "What were you trying to force instead of waiting for?"

Sometimes they responded defensively at first. But as they trained more, many of them began to soften—not in intensity, but in ego. Raw aggression turned into focus. Anger turned into strategy. Desperation turned into growth. That's when I realized:

A black belt doesn't just win rounds.

A black belt guides others toward winning within themselves—not through humiliation, but through quiet redirection.

Fighters can hit hard. Martial artists help others learn to control how they hit—and more importantly, why.

WHEN YOU BECOME THE ANCHOR OTHERS RELY ON

There's a quiet moment in a martial artist's life when you realize people no longer just look at you for technique—they look at you for steadiness.

It happens gradually. You start to notice that during intense training sessions, students glance your way, not to copy your movements, but to check your calm. When sparring gets heated or someone loses control emotionally, people look at how *you* react. If there's conflict or tension in the room, their eyes go to the black belts—to see whether they should respond with panic or patience. Without meaning to, you become an anchor.

When students doubt themselves, they ask you for reassurance—sometimes directly, sometimes just through the question in their eyes. When a technique feels out of reach, they expect you to help them navigate frustration without letting them mentally quit. When someone gets hit and feels exposed or embarrassed, they gauge your response to know whether they should feel shame or treat it as a normal part of learning.

It wasn't that I was always perfectly composed—I had my own internal battles. But I learned that leadership doesn't require never struggling. It requires not allowing struggle to shake your core values. Even when I felt unsure, I made sure I never trained like someone who was giving up internally. Even when I missed something or stumbled, I made sure to reset with intention, showing that imperfection wasn't failure unless you chose to stay there.

The longer I stayed on this path, the more I realized: People don't follow black belts because they are untouchable.
They follow black belts because they remain grounded when things get shaky.

In time, my belt stopped being something I wore because I earned it—it became something I carried because people needed me to. And carrying that weight didn't burden me. It strengthened me.

THE WEIGHT YOU CHOOSE TO CARRY WILL SHAPE WHO YOU BECOME

Responsibility didn't arrive all at once. It built gradually—through staying when others left, teaching even while still learning, remaining calm when others reacted, and holding discipline even beyond the mats. But at a certain point, I realized something important:

A black belt isn't just something you wear.
It becomes something you carry.

And what you choose to do with that weight will shape who you become.

That truth became clearer to me on my 33rd birthday. My father surprised me with a video message from Lyoto Machida—someone I had followed for years, not just because of his success in MMA, but because of the way he carried himself. He wasn't simply a fighter I admired—he was my favorite martial artist because of his composure, his calm presence under pressure, and his commitment to philosophy as much as technique. I had drawn from his mindset long before I ever saw him in person. In the video, Machida said:

"What is the best part of our professional career? When we teach someone— because we have very good tools to transform the lives of other people. It's not just about technique, but it's about the philosophy that we can put into our training and empower others." – Lyoto Machida

He could have spoken about winning titles or mastering techniques. Instead, he spoke about the deeper purpose of martial arts—teaching not just movements, but transformation. His words didn't feel like encouragement. They felt like confirmation. A reminder that being a black belt wasn't about proving skill—it was about shaping lives, starting with your own.

Sometime after that birthday, I had the honor of meeting Machida in person while working at *LFA 160*. Standing in the same space as someone whose philosophy had already influenced me, I was reminded that true martial artists don't just *say* what they believe—they live it through calm, focused presence. He carried the same quiet strength in person that he expressed in his words. That moment reinforced everything I had begun to understand:

A black belt is not an arrival. It is an agreement—
To lead without arrogance.
To teach without ego.
To grow without an ending.
To carry responsibility not as a burden, but as a calling.

I wasn't just representing myself anymore. I was representing the path. I was ready to keep carrying it. But I didn't yet know that soon, I would face a moment where responsibility wouldn't be tested by leadership, or instruction, or how I guided others—it would be tested by what happened when I could barely stand on my own. And in that season, I would learn whether my foundation was rooted deeply enough…to carry me when my body could not.

"Growth begins the moment you become willing to let go of what you think you already know."

CHAPTER VIII

The Test of Survival

✦

Injuries inside the dojo make sense. You fall wrong, take a bad hit, miscalculate a landing. At least in those moments, pain comes from a place you understand—born in a space you chose to enter. But sometimes, injury doesn't arrive in the ring, or on the mat, or during a moment of combat. Sometimes it finds you in the quiet, when you least expect it—far from a fight, but testing your warrior spirit just the same.

My severe ankle dislocation and foot fracture didn't happen during training. It happened unexpectedly, and when it did, pain surged so sharply that I knew instantly this wasn't something I could walk off. There was no bumping it out, no "shake it off and keep going." The body has a way of signaling to you when something has gone very wrong. This was one of those moments.

I was alone when it happened.

The kind of alone where no one is there to lift you up.

The kind of alone where you find out what your instinct really is.

The kind of alone where there's no audience to impress… only a question to answer:

Do you break… or do you move?

I remember the shock, the feeling of structural failure deep in my foot and ankle, the sudden realization that weight was no longer support but agony. But instinct kicked in before panic did. Not the instinct to scream—but the instinct to survive. The same warrior mindset that helped me fight through sparring rounds, tournaments, and pressure now had only one objective:

Don't collapse here.

So I moved. Not gracefully, not powerfully—just persistently.

Every motion felt like fire, but I kept going, dragging myself toward safety—not because I believed I could walk it off, but because stopping would mean surrender. Not to an opponent... but to circumstance.

Sometime after, when I received confirmation of the severity, there was no relief in having been right. There was just silence, the kind that follows impact. I had surgery within days. Movement was stripped away. I was forced into stillness. And that's when a different kind of pain set in.

A martial artist learns early to control breath through impact. But this was a different kind of impact. Not a strike to the ribs or a leg kick you could breathe through. This was paused movement. Restricted will.

I couldn't train. I couldn't spar. I couldn't express the art that had become my way of thinking, breathing, and existing. I had pushed through exhaustion before. I had sparred through bruises and soreness. But you can't push through a broken foundation. You must wait. And warriors don't wait easily.

When movement was taken from me, I wasn't just dealing with physical pain—I was battling the feeling that part of who I was had been temporarily taken, locked behind recovery and time.

But deep inside, beneath the swelling, beneath the immobilization, beneath the silence of halted training... something else remained unbroken.

I didn't know when I'd fully return. I didn't know what strength would remain afterward. But I knew one thing:

My body had been forced to stop.
My spirit hadn't.

And as long as that stayed true, this injury would not be the end of my journey—It would become the beginning of a new kind of strength.

THE BATTLE BETWEEN PAIN AND PURPOSE

The physical pain from the injury eventually dulled into something manageable, but that was when the harder fight began—the battle between who I was forced to be and who I still believed I was.

Recovery sounds simple from the outside: rest, follow the doctor's instructions, let time do its work. But for someone used to pushing through resistance, stopping feels unnatural. Not being able to move with intention felt worse than pain—it felt like being disconnected from myself.

For years, martial arts had shaped my rhythm: training, teaching, refining, evolving. But now my days were dictated not by discipline, but by limitation. Progress was no longer measured in speed, precision, or strength—but in how many degrees my ankle could rotate or how many steps I could take without collapse.

The dojo teaches you to breathe through tension—but injury teaches you to breathe through stillness.

There were days I caught myself trying to visualize drills, imagining footwork patterns I physically couldn't execute. I'd close my eyes and walk through kata or sparring rhythms in my head, hoping the mental rehearsal would keep the connection alive. But sometimes, the images felt distant—like watching someone else's body move in a way mine currently couldn't. That's when fear tried to enter.

Not fear of never walking again.

Fear of being less when I returned.

Fear of being forgotten.

Fear that while I was sitting still, others were improving.

Fear that I would lose part of what made me *"me."*

But there was another voice—quieter, but stronger the more I listened to it. It wasn't the loud warrior spirit that charged through sparring rounds or stood up after being knocked through drywall. It was calmer, deeper, more patient.

It said: *This is not a pause in who you are. It is a stage of it.*

Recovery became training—just a different kind.

Breathing became a drill.

Re-learning to stand became a technique.

Controlled movement became kata.

Patience became a sparring partner I had to learn to read, time, and respect.

And even though I couldn't train physically the way I wanted, I refused to mentally drift. The body was in recovery—but the purpose stayed alive. I wasn't losing my identity. I was guarding it through discipline in stillness.

In that quiet internal fight, I realized something profound: Not all warriors are forged in combat. Some are forged in the ability to wait without surrender.

I wasn't just preparing to move again. I was preparing to return with purpose sharpened by stillness.

THE BLUE BELT TEST: PAIN, PRIDE, AND PUSHING BEYOND LIMITS

By the time I stepped into my Brazilian Jiu-Jitsu blue belt evaluation, I had already recovered from my ankle and foot surgery and slowly worked my way back into training. My body wasn't the same as before, but my mindset had sharpened. Survival had taught me patience—but now it was time to prove that survival hadn't dulled my will to fight.

The evaluation was demanding—testing endurance, control, transitions, timing, and resilience under pressure. Somewhere during the process, during a hard sequence of grappling, I felt it—a sharp, tearing pain in my knee. Something deep, unfamiliar, and immediate. In a split second, I knew what had happened. Something was wrong. My body had sent me a clear signal again.

But this time, unlike the first injury, I wasn't alone.

There were eyes.

Expectations.

Pressure.

Pride.

And the warrior instinct rose first.

In that moment, quitting didn't feel like the smart decision—it felt like surrendering who I had become through hardship. My ankle injury had forced me to stop. This time, I still had a choice. So I made one:

I would finish.

I didn't show what happened. I pushed through the pain, controlling my reactions, operating not from comfort but from will. Every movement brought resistance from my body, but mentally, I refused to let it shake my clarity. I completed the evaluation with damage deep in my knee, not with reckless aggression, but with controlled defiance.

When I was awarded my blue belt, it didn't feel like a token of achievement. It felt like proof that pain doesn't decide your limits—purpose does. But it also wasn't a moment of ego. It wasn't "look what I overcame." It was quieter than that. It felt like saying:

I am still here. And I still choose to move.

Eventually, I had surgery for the torn meniscus. And once again, I found myself in recovery. But this time was different. I understood now that healing was not weakness nor retreat—it was part of the discipline of staying in this journey long-term.

The first injury forced me to stop and survive.

The second injury showed me that even when my body gives out, my spirit chooses how I finish the round.

THE ILLUSION OF STRENGTH AND THE REALIZATION OF HUMILITY

Pushing through the torn meniscus to finish my evaluation felt like a victory—but recovery taught me that strength isn't always about defiance. Sometimes it's about knowing when willpower must shift into wisdom.

After surgery, I was forced back into stillness again. But this time, the silence felt different. I didn't feel as lost as I had during the ankle injury. I wasn't fighting the immobility with panic, or questioning who I was without motion. Instead, I began to see recovery as part of the martial journey, not a pause from it.

Before, I believed strength meant always pushing forward, even if it meant hiding pain or proving I could push through it. But in recovery, I learned a different kind of strength—the kind that chooses discipline over recklessness, patience over panic, and long-term growth over short-term pride.

There's a temptation in martial arts, especially for those with warrior instincts, to measure toughness by how much pain you can take without showing it. But I started to understand that if strength is only expressed in defying pain, it risks becoming ego disguised as resilience.

True humility came from realizing:
- It takes courage to push through a fight.
- But it also takes wisdom to heal without rushing.
- It takes resolve to endure pain.
- But it takes maturity to prevent avoidable pain in the future.
- It takes pride to say, *"I won't quit."*
- But it takes purpose to say, *"I will recover so I can keep going."*

The first injury had tested my ability to survive.

The second tested my ability to endure with purpose.

Recovery after the second injury tested my ability to evolve with humility.

And somewhere in that process, I began to understand something profound:

I didn't want to be someone who pushed recklessly until broken—I wanted to be someone who adapted wisely to keep becoming more than I once was.

Strength without humility breaks.
Strength with humility endures.

CRAWLING TOWARD RECOVERY

This time, recovery wasn't about waiting—it was about rebuilding. I wasn't counting days until I could return to "normal"; I was working intentionally to come back stronger, smarter, and more balanced in body and mind.

The first time I was injured, I saw recovery as something I had to endure. But now, I treated it as training—just in a different form.

Where sparring once tested my reactions, physical therapy tested my patience.

Where conditioning once measured my stamina, controlled rehab measured my discipline. Where drills once refined techniques at full speed, now I focused on micro-movements—heel raises, controlled steps, small adjustments that demanded precision and control. Where before I sought intensity, now I sought mastery of rebuilding from the ground up.

I wasn't chasing a fast recovery. I was building a sustainable one. Those slow, quiet moments—stretching, strengthening, resetting— became proof that movement could still have purpose even when it wasn't explosive. I began treating each small improvement like a form of kata, flowing through whatever my current limits allowed with full attention and respect. As I progressed, I realized something powerful:

Before injury, I trained to test my limits.
After injury, I trained to extend my journey.

I wasn't racing to catch up anymore—I was preparing to stay in this longer than pain could last. And when I finally stepped back into full training, I didn't move with fear or hesitation. I moved with a new level of awareness. Every strike had more clarity. Every transition had more thought. Every moment of fatigue reminded me that I had already survived worse. I didn't return as someone struggling to reclaim who I was. I returned as someone newly aligned with who I was becoming.

INJURY AS A TEACHER

Coming back to training after injury changed not just my movements, but my mindset. I no longer saw pain simply as something to ignore or battle through. I saw it as feedback—information that could be used to build smarter, stronger, and longer-lasting technique.

I had always believed in intensity, endurance, and grit. But through injury, I learned to balance those traits with awareness, adaptability, and sustainability. Pain had once been something to conquer—now it became something to understand. That shift changed how I approached teaching as well.

Before, I pushed students based on what I believed they could handle physically. After injury, I began paying closer attention to how they were internalizing struggle. I watched how they moved when fatigue set in—not just to test will, but to identify technical breakdown before it led to unnecessary injury.

I also became more attuned to mindset. Some students tried to prove toughness the same way I once had—ignoring pain to appear unbreakable. Others grew discouraged when they didn't bounce back as fast as they hoped. I recognized those mental battles because I had faced them firsthand.

Instead of telling students simply to "push harder," I began asking questions:

- *What did you feel just before the movement broke down?*
- *Are you pushing to grow, or pushing to avoid looking weak?*
- *Are you masking pain or mastering it?*

Injury taught me that true toughness isn't shown in how long you ignore pain—it's shown in how you respond to it, how you navigate it, and how you come back from it with intention rather than desperation.

My teaching evolved from showing students *how to endure* to helping them understand *how to adapt*. I no longer saw injury as something that takes you off the warrior's path—it becomes a part of it, shaping humility, perspective, and long-term survival.

Pain had tested me.

Recovery had refined me.

Teaching through that experience completed the lesson.

And somewhere in that process, I realized something:

I wasn't just surviving the test—I was transforming through it.

THE WARRIOR STILL STANDS

There's a point in every martial artist's path when survival takes on a new meaning. It's no longer about just making it through the round or pushing past fatigue. It's about proving that even when life forces you to stop, you will still choose to continue.

After everything—the break, the surgeries, the delay, the frustration, the rebuilding—what mattered most wasn't that I resumed training. It was that I returned differently.

Injury didn't just test my physical resilience—it tested my identity. It challenged the pride that once pushed me blindly forward. It reshaped my definition of strength. It sharpened my patience, my awareness, my teaching, and my ability to separate ego from true will. I came back not simply to train—but to continue becoming.

There's something powerful about standing again after being forced to fall. Not because standing means you never broke—but because it means your spirit refused to stay down once your body healed.

When I stepped back onto the mats, I didn't see myself as someone who had been weakened by injury. I saw myself as someone who had survived a quiet war and learned from it. I didn't return just to fight again. I returned to carry forward what pain had taught me. And long before I would ever step into a cage or face the next test life would throw my way, one truth became clear:

A warrior is not defined by the absence of injury.
A warrior is defined by the decision to rise every time the body tries to convince the spirit to stay down.

The test wasn't just about survival. It was about proving that I still belonged on the path. And this time, I walked it not just to push my limits—but to honor what I had learned from breaking them.

"Pain teaches you what strength will cost. Survival teaches you how to pay for it."

CHAPTER IX

Kumite: A Test of Courage

There are moments in a martial artist's journey that feel less like competition and more like crossing a line inside yourself. For me, the day I stepped into the cage wasn't about proving I was the better fighter. It wasn't about chasing a record or building a career. It was about doing something that fear tried to convince me I had no business doing.

It was about stepping into a space that required all-in commitment—not because I was certain I would win, but because I refused to let doubt define me.

A year had passed since I recovered from my injury. I could still feel it some days—that dull, lingering reminder that my foundation had once shattered. Every step into training after recovery had been part of a quiet rebuilding, but there was still a question that lived in the back of my mind:

Am I truly back… or just functioning again?

When the opportunity to fight in the cage came, I didn't jump at it with excitement. I sat with it. I thought about the risk. I felt the old injury pulse in the background like a memory I couldn't completely outrun. But I also thought about my students—the ones who looked to me not just for technique, but for example.

I thought about every time I told them that courage wasn't the absence of fear, but the decision to act in spite of it.

If I told them to face challenges, but refused to step into one myself... What kind of black belt would I be? So I said yes.

Fight day was loud. Even before entering the cage, you can hear everything amplified—the sound of gloves being slapped together, coaches giving sharp instructions, walkout music echoing through the arena, the energy of people watching, judging, anticipating. Under the lights, everything feels both real and surreal, like the world has narrowed to one question: *will you still move forward?*

As I stood near the cage door, ready to walk in, I didn't feel arrogance or adrenaline-fueled confidence. I felt a quiet kind of clarity. My ankle still wasn't trustworthy. I knew I was stepping in against someone more experienced than me in this exact environment. This was his world. It wasn't mine. But I wasn't there to be someone I wasn't. I was there to prove that even when uncertain, I would still stand.

When the cage door opened and I stepped inside, it didn't feel like entering a fight. It felt like entering a test—not against him, but against everything I had become since the injuries, the stillness, and the rebuilding.

I wasn't there to dominate.

I was there to demonstrate.

And deep inside, before the first bell ever rang, I knew:

No matter what happened next—courage was already in motion.

THE FIGHT WITHIN THE FIGHT

The bell rang, and the energy in the cage shifted. Even when you're composed, there's something about the first exchange that makes your senses sharpen instantly. Movement becomes more deliberate. Every step, every adjustment of distance, every glance tells a story about pace, power, and pressure.

My opponent moved like someone familiar with this environment—confident, controlled, experienced. I wasn't intimidated, but I understood immediately that I was in his domain. Where others might hear the crowd or feel the pressure of lights, I felt his rhythm and how he wanted to dictate the flow.

I kept calm and stayed strategic. I didn't rush. I let my training settle in. But then—it happened. During one of the early movement exchanges, I felt something sharp twist deep in my knee.

Not a light tweak. Not discomfort.

A sudden, forceful signal—the kind that speaks in a language you learn from injury: *Something is wrong.*

For a fraction of a second, time felt suspended—not because I was in danger of being hit, but because I was in danger of reacting emotionally. Pain tries to wake up fear. Fear tries to force panic. And panic wants you to either lash out recklessly or mentally collapse.

This was the real fight. I had two choices:

- React like a wounded fighter, growing sloppy, desperate, or erratic...
- Or respond like a martial artist—aware of the pain, acknowledging it, but refusing to let it dictate my next move.

So I chose response.

I adjusted. I stabilized mentally before stabilizing physically. I controlled my breath instead of letting it spike. I shifted my stance slightly to protect what I could without broadcasting injury. The pain was real, but so was my purpose.

My opponent kept pressing, likely sensing physical resistance—but not weakness. And I made sure that what I displayed wasn't panic or aggression, but persistence.

Every strike landed after that moment required more will than power. Every step forward was a choice. The fight from that point was less about scoring points or securing dominance—and more about refusing to mentally exit the cage just because my body was compromised.

Pain became background noise. Purpose stayed in front. This wasn't about earning applause. It wasn't about silencing doubt. It was about staying composed—not for ego, but for everyone watching who needed to know that courage isn't spotless... sometimes, it limps and keeps going. I wasn't fighting to win. I was fighting to finish—as myself.

FOR THEM AND FOR ME

Somewhere in the middle of the fight—long after the knee tweak and long before the final bell—I found a strange moment of clarity. It didn't come in a sudden burst of adrenaline or some cinematic surge of power. It came in the quiet space between exchanges, when breath meets focus and instinct meets intention.

I wasn't winning in a traditional sense. My opponent was experienced, confident in this kind of arena. Every movement reminded me that he had done this before. But even as he pressed the pace, I noticed something important: I was still there. Even hurt, even tested, I hadn't mentally broken or emotionally folded. I hadn't turned desperate, reckless, or afraid.

I was still *responding*.

In that moment, I remembered why I had said yes in the first place. My students needed to see that courage isn't always defined by victory. That stepping in matters. That staying calm in discomfort matters. That finishing matters—not because you are unbreakable, but because your spirit refuses to exit even when your body protests.

This wasn't a display of dominance.

It was a display of presence.

I wanted them to see that martial arts isn't about being fearless—it's about standing willingly in the presence of fear and making conscious choices anyway. I wanted them to see that pain doesn't have to cause panic, and that pressure doesn't have to create chaos. And somewhere in that storm, I realized I wasn't just doing this for them.

I was doing it for me.

Because there's a moment after injury, recovery, and rebuilding when you must answer a personal question:

Am I still capable of stepping into fire with intention?

Not to outperform others—but to prove that I still belong in the arena of challenge.

The fight went on. My knee hurt. My ankle, though stable, reminded me of past damage. The strikes exchanged weren't perfect. My performance wasn't polished. But I was still in control of one thing:

My composure.

And that was enough.

When you fight under those conditions, you stop measuring success by how many strikes you land. You start measuring it by how deeply you remain aligned with your purpose while pain tries to pull you away from it. This wasn't about winning the cage. It was about proving I could enter and leave it unchanged in spirit.

AFTER THE BELL

When the bell finally rang, there wasn't a sense of glory. There wasn't a dramatic celebration or a crushing sense of defeat. There was silence in my mind—the kind that comes only when everything has been stripped down to its essence.

I walked out of the cage slower than I had entered, not from exhaustion alone, but from the weight of what the moment meant. My body ached—the knee, the ankle, the fatigue that seeps in after adrenaline fades. But there was peace behind it all. A peace born from honesty. I had faced the one opponent that can't be avoided—the self that doubts.

And I had answered.

The crowd's noise became background again. My mind wasn't on how the fight looked or what anyone thought of it. I wasn't trying to replay exchanges or second-guess what I could've done better. What mattered was simple: I didn't quit. I didn't lose myself. I stayed composed.

I didn't walk away with a title. I walked away with something more important:

- I had proven my resilience to myself.
- I had learned that even in adversity, I could remain aligned with my philosophy.
- I had affirmed that my journey wasn't about perfection—it was about persistence with purpose.

When you walk out of an experience like that, you see everything differently—not because the world changes, but because you've proven something to yourself that can't be taught in class. You've carried your pain into fire and come back with your integrity intact.

That night, my students saw me not as untouchable, but as human—someone who struggled, endured, and chose to continue. That lesson meant more to me than any trophy could have.

In the days after, I noticed the small things again—the weight of the gloves, the way the mat feels under bare feet, the quiet of an empty dojo after class. Every sound, every movement, every breath seemed more alive. I realized that martial arts was never meant to protect us from pain. It was meant to teach us how to move through it with grace.

I didn't step into the cage to become something.

I stepped in to confirm that despite everything I had gone through—I still was. And when the door closed behind me that night, I carried forward a truth I now teach my students:

"Courage isn't the absence of pain or fear—it's the decision to stand in both and keep your posture."

*"The warrior's duty is not to conquer others,
but to master the moment they stand in."*

CHAPTER X

A Warrior's Duty

When I stepped out of the cage and into the silence that followed, I didn't feel bigger. I didn't feel like I had leveled up or claimed some new title. What I felt was weight—but not the kind that crushes you. The kind you choose to carry.

People who knew the extent of my injuries, the ones who had seen my recovery day-by-day, offered genuine praise. They weren't celebrating a win; they were acknowledging the fight within the fight—the internal one that doesn't show up on scorecards. Their respect didn't inflate me. It grounded me.

Because when people look at you with belief—not because you're unbeatable, but because you refuse to disappear under pressure—that belief becomes something you feel responsible for.

Stepping into the cage had never been about victory; stepping out of it gave me clarity.

I could still endure.

I could still choose courage when it cost something.

I could still set an example my students could look to—not of perfection, but of perseverance.

And that realization didn't make me feel proud. It made me feel accountable.

Being a warrior isn't about stacking accomplishments. It's about what you do with what you've survived. It's about being aware that others may follow your footsteps not because they're forced to—but because they trust the way you walk.

That's when the concept of duty shifted for me.

There's a Japanese saying:

"Bushido wa jin ni ari"—*"The warrior's path is found in compassion."*

At first, I didn't fully understand how compassion belonged beside combat, but over time I realized this:

Strength that serves only the self is just power. Strength that lifts others becomes purpose.

It wasn't something assigned because of rank or years of experience. It wasn't an obligation pushed onto my shoulders. It was something I accepted willingly, with a clearer sense of who I needed to be going forward. It wasn't a burden of being better than others. It was the responsibility of being consistent *for* others. To push when necessary—not just harder, but smarter. To teach not only what I knew, but what was forged through struggle. To lead by example—not just in strength, but in restraint. To stand not above students, but ahead of fear—so they could see that it's survivable.

Duty didn't feel heavy. It felt like direction. And for the first time, I didn't feel like I was fighting to belong on the path. I felt like I was prepared to help others keep walking it.

FIGHTING FOR OTHERS, NOT AGAINST THEM

After the cage experience, I didn't feel the urge to prove myself to opponents. Instead, I felt a stronger responsibility to those who trained under me. My battles were no longer about winning clashes—they were about helping students break through their own limitations, doubts, and fears.

Before, I taught with intensity. I pushed students hard because I believed struggle forged strength. That part didn't change. But *how* I pushed them did.

I stopped pushing from a place of expectation—
and started pushing from a place of understanding.

I knew what it was like to feel pain and hide it. I knew what it was like to question if I still belonged on the mat. I knew what it meant to step forward with a compromised body and an uncertain mind.

So when a student hesitated during sparring, I no longer saw hesitation as weakness—I saw it as an unspoken question: *"Can I handle this?"* When someone failed a drill repeatedly, I stopped thinking they weren't trying hard enough—I wondered if they were afraid of being seen trying and still failing. When a student panicked under pressure, I didn't just teach technique—I talked to them about breathing, grounding, and responding instead of reacting.

Because I had lived those moments—not as theory, but as reality.
I came to understand something important:

Some people fight to dominate.
Some fight to survive.

A warrior fights to protect—and protection doesn't always come from stopping someone else. Sometimes it comes from helping someone stand stronger within themselves. That became my mission inside the dojo.

I didn't need to fight *against* anyone. I needed to fight *for* those who were still learning to believe in themselves.

And that shift changed everything. I wasn't shaping fighters—I was trying to forge martial artists who understood that strength without control is reckless, and control without purpose is empty.

Teaching became a continuation of my journey, not a separate act. Every time a student overcame fear, stood taller after doubt, or chose discipline over frustration—I felt the same quiet affirmation I did when stepping out of the cage:

I'm still walking the path.
Only now, I'm helping others find their footing on it too.

WHAT IT MEANS TO CARRY A LEGACY

Duty feels different when you realize you aren't walking alone—but also not entirely in someone else's footsteps. I didn't create the path I started on. I was born into it.

Davis Karate wasn't just a place I trained—it was the foundation of who I became. I grew up under the roof of a dojo that my father built with hard work, respect, and a firm belief that martial arts wasn't just about physical ability—it was a way to shape character.

I had watched my father not just teach, but *lead*. I had seen black belts and instructors from different places respect him—not because of fear or rank, but because of how he carried himself. I saw students return year after year, not because they were chasing belts, but because what they learned inside that dojo changed what they believed they could handle outside of it.

As a child, I didn't fully understand what it meant to come from a martial arts lineage. I just knew I was expected to give my best. But as I grew older and began teaching, especially after facing injury and the cage, I saw things differently.

I realized that carrying a legacy doesn't mean copying it.
It means protecting its spirit while helping it evolve.

Some students came in wanting to fight. Others wanted to find confidence. Some were searching for discipline, others for belonging. The next generation wasn't always motivated by the same values or fears that older generations had. And if I tried to lead them using only the methods of the past, I risked losing them before they ever understood what martial arts could truly offer them. So I stopped trying to force students to fit into the legacy. I began shaping the legacy to reach the students.

That didn't mean abandoning the roots—it meant honoring them by making sure they could keep growing. The foundation of our art remained the same:

Respect, humility, perseverance, discipline, and self-control.

But the way we applied those principles grew to include expanded striking methods, Brazilian Jiu-Jitsu, broader integration of combat concepts, mindset training, and a better understanding of mental resilience.

Some traditions are worth preserving. Others are meant to evolve— not to weaken the art, but to ensure it stays alive for those who need it today. I didn't inherit a dojo just to keep it the same.
I inherited a duty to keep it strong enough to survive new challenges— just as I had. Legacy, I realized, isn't about repeating the past.
It's about ensuring the path still leads forward.

DISCIPLINE WITHOUT RECOGNITION

There's a part of martial arts that people rarely talk about—not because it's secret, but because it's not glamorous. It's not the big wins, the belts, the cage fights, or the public displays. It's what happens when no one is watching.

Stepping into the cage was a moment people saw.

Showing up day after day afterward, whether anyone noticed or not, was where duty truly lived.

It's easy to give your best when people are cheering. It's much harder to do it when the room is empty, the mirror is your only audience, and the voice inside asks whether this effort still matters. But that's where real discipline exists.

Waking up tired but still training because consistency matters. Correcting your own technique even when no one will point it out. Leading warm-ups with the same energy whether five students show up or fifty. Fixing your posture mid-kata because your standard is higher than your mood. Choosing patience with a struggling student instead of rushing for a cleaner class flow. Repeating drills that no one applauds you for.

These things don't get likes, belts, or highlight reels. They don't create hype. They build character.

Over time, I learned that leadership isn't just what you say or do in front of others—it's what you hold yourself accountable to when you could easily get away with cutting corners. A warrior's duty isn't found in being impressive. It's found in being consistent.

Some people are motivated by recognition. But duty is tested most when recognition disappears and effort must still remain. A warrior doesn't train for applause, because applause doesn't last. But discipline stays with you long after the crowd forgets.

What students eventually come to respect most is not what you did once in a big moment—it's the fact that you continue to show up, fully present, again and again, even when the world is silent.

Because consistency builds trust.

And trust builds legacy.

LIVING AS PROOF, NOT A PERFORMER

As my responsibility deepened, I became more aware of a quiet truth: students don't just learn from what you teach—they learn from what you consistently live.

Anyone can act disciplined for an hour. Anyone can say the right things in class. Anyone can sound philosophical when things are going well. But students notice who remains calm under pressure. They notice who trains hard even when not being tested. They notice who still moves with intention after they've already achieved rank. They notice whether you speak about humility but walk with ego—or truly carry quiet respect in daily actions.

I realized that my influence as a martial artist had less to do with the belt I wore or the titles I'd earned, and more to do with the way I treated people, the way I handled setbacks, and the way I carried myself when things didn't go my way. Winning a fight doesn't mean much if you lose respect outside of it. Holding a black belt doesn't matter if you can't hold composure in conflict.

Teaching self-control means little if your own emotions are easily triggered. Talking about perseverance is empty if you crumble when challenges arise.

Students may not always remember the combinations you drill—but they remember how you responded when someone made a mistake, when someone was afraid, when someone fell behind, or when someone challenged your patience. That's when I fully understood:

I wasn't just teaching martial arts. I was demonstrating what it looks like to live them.

Not just in the dojo—but in how I approached recovery, how I carried myself under scrutiny, how I navigated exhaustion, and even in how I treated those who weren't on the same level yet.

A warrior's duty is not to perform greatness—it is to embody it quietly enough that others feel they can rise, too. So I stopped asking myself,

"How can I impress others with what I know?"

And started asking,

"How can I carry myself in a way that others feel more capable because of how I lead?"

The goal was no longer to be untouchable.
It was to be real—and still unshaken.
Not flashy—but steady.
Not above others—but ahead, clearing the path.
Because in the end, a warrior doesn't exist to stand on a pedestal.
A warrior exists to stand for something.

A QUIET OATH

There was no ceremony, no vow spoken aloud. No symbolic moment where I declared that I had taken on a new role. But somewhere along the way—after the injuries, after rebuilding, after the cage, after watching students transform not because I demanded greatness, but because I believed they could reach it—I made a quiet decision.

I chose duty. Not the kind that expects praise, or recognition, or prestige. But the kind that carries weight with humility. The kind that walks forward even when no one is watching. The kind that lives the art beyond the mat.

I didn't swear to be flawless.

I didn't promise to always have the right answer.

I didn't vow to never struggle again.

But I did commit to continuing—to keep becoming, to keep evolving, to stay grounded in the path whether it led to victory or challenge.

I committed to standing steady so my students could find their footing. I committed to being honest about pain so others would know recovery was possible. I committed to not just wearing a belt, but honoring what it represented through action. I committed to showing that strength is not loud, anger is not power, and courage is not perfection.

I chose to be the kind of warrior who doesn't fight to prove something—but to protect something. I don't need everyone to understand why I still train or why I still teach. I just need to live in a way that proves the path matters.

A warrior's duty isn't a burden.

It is a direction.

And I walk it not because I've arrived—but because I know there is always more to become.

"There is no finish line on the Way—only the next step."

CHAPTER XI

Becoming, Not Arriving

When I was younger, I believed there would be a point where everything would make sense—where I would feel complete as a martial artist. I didn't know exactly what that moment would look like, but I imagined it would come with a title, or a rank, or a moment of recognition that would confirm: *You've made it.*

Maybe it would be the first-degree black belt.

Maybe it would be proving I could step into the cage.

Maybe it would be earning respect from students or peers.

But each time I reached a new milestone, something surprising happened—I didn't feel finished. I didn't feel like I'd arrived anywhere. Instead, I became aware of how much more there still was to learn, refine, unlearn, rebuild, and rediscover.

The black belt didn't feel like an end. It felt like permission to finally learn seriously. The cage wasn't proof of mastery. It was a test of whether I could walk into fear willingly. Teaching wasn't a sign that I had all the answers—it was a constant reminder of how much I still needed to explore, especially when students asked questions that forced me to go deeper.

Each achievement opened the door to a longer hallway I couldn't see the end of. That used to frustrate me. I thought:

Will I ever feel like I've "made it"?

Will there ever be a moment where I feel complete, unquestioned, fully arrived?

It took time—and humility—to understand something essential:

Arrival is an illusion created by impatience.

There is no final rank that completes you.
No single fight that defines you.
No one moment that cements your legacy.
No belt that makes you untouchable.
Every level only expands your awareness of what's beyond it.
You don't stop growing because you've reached a destination.
You grow because you accept that there isn't one.
When I let go of the need to arrive, I became free to keep becoming.

HOW GROWTH QUIETY RESETS

One of the most humbling things about growth is that it doesn't announce itself as completion—it resets your perspective instead. Every time I advanced, whether through skill, rank, or personal growth, I didn't feel like I reached the top of something. I felt like I had just taken the first real step into a deeper level of understanding.

It's like climbing a mountain, believing you're nearing the peak, only to reach a ridge and realize there's an entirely new range stretching beyond your view. You're not at the end—you're simply at a vantage point you couldn't see before.

That's what earning my black belt felt like.

That's what healing from injury felt like.

That's what stepping into the cage felt like.

That's what leading others through their own doubts felt like.

Each experience expanded my awareness of what was still ahead. Before, knowledge felt like something to acquire. Eventually, it became something to refine, break down, reexamine, and often learn again from a more mature mindset. Techniques I once executed with raw intensity now demanded efficiency and precision. Lessons I once taught from confidence I now taught from careful awareness of how each student absorbed struggle differently. Growth didn't make things easier. It made me more aware of how much further I could go.

In some ways, that used to feel overwhelming—as if there was no finish line to chase, no final proof of mastery to reach. But in time, I began to see the beauty in that reality. When you think there's an end, you rush. When you understand the path is ongoing, you walk with better posture.

In martial arts, there's a term often used: *shoshin*, a "beginner's mind." It doesn't mean forgetting what you know—it means staying open to learning as though everything still has something to teach you.

I didn't lose confidence as I deepened in skill—I simply lost the illusion that confidence required certainty. I stopped training to feel finished. I started training to remain capable of evolving. Growth resets you not to weaken you, but to remind you that becoming is a living state, not a one-time event.

REINVENTION AS A LIFESTYLE

As I grew older in the arts, I noticed a shift in how I viewed evolution. Early on, change felt like something forced by circumstance— switching styles when exposed to new systems, or adapting because competition demanded it. But over time, I stopped reacting to change and started embracing it as part of my identity as a martial artist.

Reinvention became less of a crisis and more of a practice. When I moved away from home and found myself training in places where traditions were different, I didn't feel like I was betraying my roots. I felt like I was expanding on them. Working with a professional boxer didn't make me abandon my foundation—it made me refine the way I moved, timed, and thought. It opened my eyes to rhythms and strategies I hadn't fully explored before.

Training alongside practitioners of Aikido, Jiu-Jitsu, and kickboxing didn't dilute who I was—it distilled me further into something more complete.

I wasn't changing styles to become someone new.

I was evolving to become more fully myself.

Over time, my technique became less about which style it came from and more about what felt true to my purpose, my body, and my understanding of timing, control, and intent. Teaching evolved too. I didn't teach solely the way I was taught—I began incorporating what I had personally learned through growth, injury, pressure, and real application.

And even injury played a role in evolution. My reconstructed ankle changed the way I stepped. My knee surgery affected how I planted, angled, and transitioned. Instead of resisting these changes, I embraced them—reforming technique around what my body could now sustain, which in turn made my teachings more adaptable for students of different builds, limitations, and strengths. Some see reinvention as starting over. I came to see it as sharpening what already existed. The more I evolved, the more I understood:

Martial arts isn't about proving how much of the old you can cling to. It's about discovering how much of the new you're willing to grow into.

Reinvention, when accepted willingly, became not a sign of instability—but a measure of maturity. Because when becoming is your path, change is not a threat. It is the way forward.

LIVING THE PROCESS

There was a quiet shift in me when I finally stopped measuring my journey by milestones. I didn't stop achieving. I didn't stop setting goals. But I no longer confused achievement with completion.

Instead of asking, *"When will I get there?"*

I started asking, *"How deeply can I live here?"*

Whether I was training, teaching, recovering, or learning something new, I no longer saw these as stages moving me toward a finish line. They became states of being that were equally important, equally valid, equally part of who I was becoming. Not every day was meant to be a breakthrough. Some days were meant for maintenance. Some for rebuilding. Some for refining subtle details no one else would notice. Some simply for showing up and reinforcing discipline.

Before, I looked for signs that I was "advancing." I looked for moments that confirmed I was progressing quickly enough. After letting go of arrival, I learned to value immersion over advancement. Progress didn't have to look like elevation—it could look like deepening.

That shift made me more patient with my journey and more present with my students. I wasn't trying to force growth to happen faster than it was meant to. I was fully engaging in the process with an open mind, knowing that every rep, every conversation, every correction, every injury lesson, every moment of doubt worked as a refinement tool.

The path didn't feel endless in a discouraging way. It felt expansive—like a river I wasn't racing across but flowing with.

There is peace in realizing there is no final version of who you're supposed to be. There is only the version you are today, shaped by what you've survived, learned, let go of, and embraced.

Becoming isn't a checkpoint you pass—it's the rhythm you walk in. And for the first time, I no longer feared that I might not "arrive." I was content knowing I was becoming—and that was always enough.

THE PATH AS IDENTITY

There was a time when I trained to achieve.

Then I trained to recover.

Then I trained to prove.

But now, I train because it is part of who I am.

Some people see martial arts as something they *do*. I came to understand that for me, it had become something I *am*. Not because I wear a belt. Not because I've competed. Not even because I teach. But because the journey has reshaped how I think, breathe, fight, fail, grow, recover, and rise.

When becoming is your way of life, the path stops being something you're trying to conquer. It becomes something you walk daily—with humility, presence, and quiet conviction.

I no longer ask myself, *"How far have I come?"*

I ask, *"How honestly am I walking the way right now?"*

Not every day is perfect. Not every season is triumphant. But none of that threatens my identity. Because identity is no longer tied to performance—it's tied to direction. I am not who I was when I earned my first belt. I am not only who I was when I stepped into the cage. And I will not be who I am today ten years from now. But every version of me will be walking the same path—steady, evolving, unfinished by choice.

Becoming is not a phase. It is a lifestyle.

Arrival is not a destination. It is a limitation.

And I have no interest in being finished.

CHAPTER XII
Teaching Beyond the Dojo

When class ends and the mats are swept clean, most people assume teaching is paused until the next session. But I began to understand that real teaching continues long after the bow, and often in moments where there are no uniforms, no rank systems, no structured drills—only life.

Some students carried lessons into school when facing bullies or academic pressure. Some applied discipline from training when dealing with family struggles, anxiety, or difficult decisions. Some used breathing control not in sparring, but in moments of anger or heartbreak. Some began to stand taller—not because they mastered a kata, but because they recognized their own worth.

That's when I realized that what I taught wasn't limited to strikes and submissions. I was helping people learn how to stand up to their own doubts, how to hold composure when life pressed them, how to find their center when everything else felt unstable. Technique may have brought them into the dojo, but what stayed with them wasn't just movement—it was mindset.

When I saw a student handle frustration better over time, I saw progress. When I noticed a timid student start speaking more confidently, I saw growth. When a student who once panicked began to find rhythm under pressure, I saw transformation.

It became clear that a true teacher is not defined by how many students win tournaments or achieve black belts. A true teacher is measured by how many students become better versions of themselves—whether they keep training or not. The dojo became a starting point, not the full scope of impact. Lessons didn't stop when class ended—they simply changed form.

NOT EVERYONE WALKS THE WAY

Over time, I learned something difficult but necessary as a teacher. Not every student who enters the dojo is ready to walk the way. Some came for exercise. Some came for confidence. Some came for rank or recognition. Some came with a competitive mindset but no desire for deeper discipline. Some simply came because someone else wanted them to—a parent, a friend, a partner.

There's nothing wrong with any of those reasons. Every journey has a starting point. But there is a transition that not everyone is willing to make. At some point, martial arts stops being something you *do* and starts becoming something that challenges who you are. That's when some students quietly fade away—not because they failed, but because they weren't ready to confront what the journey was beginning to demand of them:

Patience when they wanted shortcuts.
Humility when they preferred validation.
Repetition when they craved novelty.
Discomfort when they preferred ease.

Corrections when they only wanted praise. Purpose when they were focused on outcome. Some students loved martial arts until martial arts asked them to let go of ego.

Until the path asked them to become teachable again.
Until improvement required surrendering pride.
Until growth felt like starting over.
Until "good" was no longer enough.

That's when some step away.

I used to take it personally. I questioned whether I had failed them. I pushed harder, hoping to keep them engaged. Eventually, I understood—you cannot force someone to walk a path their spirit hasn't accepted yet.

A teacher can open the door, but walking through it is always a choice. And strangely, I found peace in that. Because the way must be chosen, not imposed. Some may leave and never return. Some may return years later, ready for more than just motion. Some never fully leave—they carry part of the journey with them, quietly growing in ways I may never see.

Not everyone stays.

Not everyone goes the distance.

But for those who do...

The path transforms from practice—into identity.

THE REQUIREMENT OF THE EMPTY CUP

There's a saying in martial arts that many people hear, but only a few truly understand:

"You cannot fill a cup that is already full."

In the beginning, most students think this refers to people with big egos—those who believe they already know everything. And yes, sometimes that's true. But over time, I realized something deeper:
A full cup isn't always filled with arrogance.
Sometimes it's filled with fear.
Sometimes with doubt.
Sometimes with insecurity.
Sometimes with fixed expectations of how progress should look like.

Sometimes with comparisons to others.

Sometimes with the belief that they must constantly appear strong.

To empty the cup means to release what is holding you back—not just pride, but also the mental noise that prevents you from fully receiving growth.

Students who thrive are rarely the ones who are the strongest at first. They are the ones who learn how to make room inside themselves for change. They are willing to be corrected without becoming defensive. They are open to repetition without growing impatient. They accept that new levels may require them to feel like beginners again. They don't cling to titles or rely on past victories.

They ask questions not to challenge authority, but to deepen understanding. And perhaps most importantly:

They do not mistake temporary struggle for failure.

Those who stay on the way are those willing to constantly empty themselves—of ego, fear, comparison, and preconceptions—so that new strength, wisdom, and awareness can fill the space that remains. Not everyone is ready for that. But for those who are, teaching becomes more than instruction—it becomes a shared journey. Because when a student empties their cup and shows up ready to grow, they are no longer just receiving the art. They are beginning to *inherit* it.

TRANSFORMING LIVES WITHOUT CREDIT

As I continued teaching, I realized something humbling: you don't always see the impact you make. Some students train for months or years and then leave without a word. You wonder if anything truly reached them. Maybe they quit because it got too hard. Maybe life pulled them in a different direction. Maybe they were searching for something martial arts couldn't give them at that time. Sometimes, it feels like your effort fell silent. But then, years later, one of them messages you unexpectedly:

"I still remember when you taught me not to panic when I felt trapped. It helped me during a hard time in my life."

"I still hear your voice reminding me to breathe before reacting."

"I didn't understand the lessons back then, but I do now."

Or you see them carry themselves differently—in their workplace, in how they parent, in how they respond to adversity. They may never mention the dojo again, yet something about their posture, their resilience, their calm presence feels familiar.

Not every student will thank you.

Not every student will stay forever.

Not every lesson will bloom under your watch.

But that's the nature of true teaching—it works in silence long after class is over. A teacher driven by recognition burns out when applause fades. A teacher driven by purpose understands that transformation often grows unnoticed. Sometimes we teach seeds, not flowers.
Sometimes we witness growth, other times we trust it. That's when I understood:

I was not teaching to be remembered.
I was teaching to help others remember themselves.

BEYOND TITLES, BEYOND WALLS

At some point, I stopped thinking of myself as just an instructor at the dojo. I realized that if martial arts had truly become part of who I was, then my responsibility to live it didn't end when I left the mat.

The title of "sensei" or "coach" may apply within a class setting, but the role of teacher—when accepted fully—travels with you everywhere.

It's there in how you respond when someone disrespects you. It's there in how you handle stress when things go wrong. It's there in how you speak to people who are unsure of themselves. It's there in whether you act with humility when praised, and integrity when unnoticed. It's there in how your children or younger students see you react in everyday life. It's there when someone who barely knows you watches how you hold your composure during conflict.

Teaching stops being about the belt around your waist and becomes about the way you carry your character. Students may forget a specific drill, but they will remember whether you walked with dignity. They may not recall a technique breakdown months later, but they will remember how you stayed calm when others were panicked. They may leave the dojo and train elsewhere, but they carry the lessons of how you treated people, how you stood firm in values, and how you embraced growth without ego.

The dojo is where martial arts are taught. Life is where they are revealed. Teaching beyond the dojo means that your actions remain a silent curriculum long after the formal lesson ends. You are not teaching to be followed—you are demonstrating a way of moving through the world so others can see what resilience, respect, and self-control look like in motion.

At this stage, you are no longer teaching students only how to throw a strike or apply a submission. You are teaching them how to stand firm in hardship, how to respond instead of react, how to evolve without losing humility. You may not always realize who is watching, learning, or being shaped by your presence. But if the way truly lives in you, teaching will continue wherever you stand.

PASSING THE FLAME, NOT THE BELT

There was a time when I believed a black belt represented the highest form of a student's journey. Now, I see it differently. Belts recognize progress—but they don't guarantee purpose. They mark levels of skill—but not always levels of understanding.

A belt can be worn.

A flame must be carried.

I realized that my role was not to create students who simply repeated what I taught, but to ignite something within them—a fire that would keep them growing long after I stopped leading them. True teaching isn't about producing duplicates. It's about helping others discover their own strength, voice, and way.

Some students may one day outrank me in different areas of training. Some may surpass me in certain skills. Some may go further in competition. Some may even evolve philosophies that branch in new directions. If I have done my job right, I won't feel threatened by that—I'll feel proud.

Because a legacy is not a cage meant to keep the next generation inside. It is a fire meant to light their way forward. Passing the flame means understanding that true leadership is not about keeping others dependent—it's about empowering them to walk confidently without you.

It also means recognizing that, just as my father passed down principles through his own example, I now carry that same responsibility—not to replicate his exact steps, but to honor the direction and spirit of the way he set in motion.

And one day, others will do the same—not because they are forced to carry the path forward, but because they choose to. When a student no longer trains out of obligation but walks the way from within, that's when the flame has truly been passed.

It's not about the belt they wear in that moment.

It's about the clarity in their eyes, the composure in their struggle, and the steadiness in their purpose.

That's when I know I haven't just taught someone how to fight... I've helped them discover how to keep becoming.

And that's when I finally understood: a belt can close a chapter, but it can never finish the story. The way is carried forward not by rank, not by reputation, but by the people we've helped stand taller than they were before. My greatest work will never be measured by what I achieved— but by what continues long after me. When a student moves forward with purpose that is truly their own, that is the moment I know the flame has been entrusted well.

Because becoming doesn't end at mastery.

It continues every time someone chooses to walk the way.

The Way Continues

I still teach today at Davis Karate, in the same place where my journey began. Some evenings, when the mats settle beneath my feet and students line up with nervous energy or quiet determination, I feel the past and present meet. I remember being the kid who trained on carpet laid thin over concrete, convinced that endurance was proof of power. I remember the injuries that tried to stop me, the test that pushed me, the students who challenged me, and the moments that reshaped me. And still, I stand—not because I have arrived, but because I continue.

My ankle still reminds me of what it once endured. Some mornings, it speaks before my mind fully wakes. But I don't resent it. It isn't a weakness—it's a signature from a chapter that formed me. It reminds me that strength isn't being untouched; strength is choosing to keep walking, even when the road carries memory.

As I move through each class, I see parts of myself in different students—some confident, some hesitant, some trying to prove themselves, others simply searching for who they are. I know not all will stay. Not everyone empties their cup. Not everyone walks the path long enough for the philosophy to sink deeper than technique. But for those who do continue, something shifts—not in a single moment, but quietly, steadily, like a spark that learns to breathe.

I used to believe the path was about reaching a point where I could finally say, "I made it." Now I understand that becoming isn't something you finish—it's something you live. I no longer train to arrive. I train to remain awake to the process of growth. And I teach not to create followers, but to help others find their own way of walking forward.

My father began this legacy, and I carry it not by repeating it step for step, but by letting it live through me and evolve through those who come after. One day, others will lead with their own voices—shaped by their trials, their growth, their tests of survival. When that happens, I'll know the way has continued exactly as it should: not held, but passed on.

The journey never promised comfort. It promised transformation. And transformation is rarely neat, never perfect, but always meaningful when walked with humility, discipline, and heart.

I don't know exactly who I'll be ten years from now. But I know this: I will still be walking. I will still be learning. I will still be teaching—not just in the dojo, but in how I carry myself through every moment that calls for intention.

Because the way is not a destination.
It's a direction.

And I am still moving forward.

A Note to the Students

To every student who has ever stepped onto the mat with me—thank you again.

You may not realize it, but each of you has shaped this journey in ways I could never have predicted. Your effort, your questions, your mistakes, your breakthroughs—they've all challenged me to grow, to learn, and to teach with more patience and purpose than the day before.

Some of my favorite moments as an instructor have been watching your growth—seeing the change from the day you first walked through the door to the student you've become. The smallest improvements, the renewed confidence, the moments when something finally *clicks*—those are the memories I carry with me.

I know some of you will go on to earn your black belt, and some of you won't. But that has never been the measure of your success to me. What matters is that you take the lessons we shared together—the discipline, the humility, the courage, the resilience—and carry them into every part of your life, long after the mat fades behind you.

I wrote this book to share the lessons that helped shape me, but the truth is, many of those lessons were strengthened because of you. Watching you struggle, improve, fall down, stand back up, and become stronger—physically and within yourselves—has reminded me, time and time again, why the Way matters.

If you carry anything from these pages, let it be this:
Growth doesn't come from perfection. It comes from showing up—especially on the days when it's hard. The Way isn't a place we arrive; it's something we choose, step by step, moment by moment.

Thank you for allowing me to be part of your path.
You've been an unforgettable part of mine.

— Tristan

About the Author

Tristan Davis is a 5th Dan martial artist and instructor at Davis Karate in Morehead, Kentucky. Raised in the art from childhood, he has spent over two decades training, teaching, and exploring the deeper lessons behind technique. His focus is not only on skill, but on character—on how we move, carry ourselves, and grow through the challenges life places before us.

As both a teacher and father, he believes that martial arts is not something we perform—it is something we *live*. The Way is practiced in stillness, in discipline, in patience, and in how we choose to meet the world each day. He continues to teach, train, and guide students of all ages.

"Lead with strength. Teach with patience. Grow with purpose. The Way continues — for you, and for those who follow your steps."